The Constitution of the United States

A LOOK AT THE NINETEENTH AMENDMENT

WOMEN WIN THE RIGHT TO VOTE

HELEN KOUTRAS BOZONELIS

MyReportLinks.com Books

an imprint of

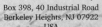

Enslow Publishers, Inc.

Box 398, 40 Industrial Road
Berkeley Heights, NJ 07922
USA

*To the amazing women in my life: Lia, Evangelia, Penelope, Marion,
Lillian, and Helen S.B.; and the men: Theodore and Justin.*

MyReportLinks.com Books, an imprint of Enslow Publishers, Inc. MyReportLinks®
is a registered trademark of Enslow Publishers, Inc.

Copyright © 2009 by Enslow Publishers, Inc.

Library of Congress Cataloging-in-Publication Data

Bozonelis, Helen Koutras.
  A Look At The Nineteenth Amendment: Women Win The Right To Vote / Helen
Koutras Bozonelis.
      p. cm. — (The Constitution of the United States)
  Includes bibliographical references and index.
  ISBN-13: 978-1-59845-067-5 (hardcover)
  ISBN-10: 1-59845-067-0 (hardcover)
  1. United States. Constitution. 19th Amendment—History—Juvenile literature. 2.
Women—Suffrage—United States—History—Juvenile literature. 3. Women—
Suffrage—United States—Juvenile literature. I. Title.
KF4895.Z9B69 2007
342.73'072—dc22
                                        2007009876

Printed in the United States of America

10 9 8 7 6 5 4 3 2 1

To Our Readers:
Through the purchase of this book, you and your library gain access to the Report Links that specifically back
up this book.
The Publisher will provide access to the Report Links that back up this book and will keep these Report Links
up to date on **www.myreportlinks.com** for five years from the book's first publication date.
We have done our best to make sure all Internet addresses in this book were active and appropriate when we
went to press. However, the author and the Publisher have no control over, and assume no liability for, the
material available on those Internet sites or on other Web sites they may link to.
The usage of the MyReportLinks.com Books Web site is subject to the terms and conditions stated on the Usage
Policy Statement on **www.myreportlinks.com**.
A password may be required to access the Report Links that back up this book. The password is found on the
bottom of page 4 of this book.
Any comments or suggestions can be sent by e-mail to comments@myreportlinks.com or to the address on the
back cover.

♻ Enslow Publishers, Inc. is committed to printing our books on recycled paper. The paper in every book contains between 10% to 30% post-consumer waste (PCW). The cover board on the outside of each book contains
100% PCW. Our goal is to do our part to help young people and the environment too!

Photo Credits: AlicePaul.org, p. 40; American Civil Liberties Union, p. 16; AP/Wide World Photos, pp. 94, 100;
Barnard Center for Research on Women, p. 99; CaseLaw.lp.FindLaw.com, p. 58; Cornell University Law School,
p. 67; EqualRightsAmendment.org, p. 98; Gale.Cengage.com, p. 75; League of Women Voters, p. 97; Library of
Congress, pp. 9, 14, 65, 77; Library of Congress, Manuscript Division, pp. 8, 11, 46, 47, 50; Library of Congress
Prints and Photographs Division, pp. 24, 28, 34, 41, 44, 45, 52, 55, 56, 61, 81; Library of Congress Rare Book and
Special Collections Division, p. 43; MyReportLinks.com Books, p. 4; National Archives, p. 87; National Park Service,
pp. 18, 92; National Organization For Women, p. 101; National Women's History Museum, p. 93; National Women's
History Project, p. 89; The New York Times, p. 102; Old-picture.com, p. 51; PBS.org, pp. 12, 84; PBSKids.org,
p. 38; Pomona College, p. 20; Shutterstock, pp. 72, 104, 105; Suffragist.com, p. 22; SusanBAnthonyHouse.org,
p. 25; University of Minnesota, p. 73; University of Missouri-Kansas City, p. 74; University of Rochester, p. 26;
University of Virginia, p. 32; U.S. Department of Justice, p. 85; WomenInCongress.House.gov, p. 103.

Cover Photo and Description: Library of Congress, Manuscript Division: Suffragists picket in front of the
White House in 1917.

CONTENTS

MyReportLinks.com Books
Great Books, Great Links, Great for Research!

The Internet sites featured in this book can save you hours of research time. These Internet sites—we call them **"Report Links"**—are constantly changing, but we keep them up to date on our Web site.

When you see this "Approved Web Site" logo, you will know that we are directing you to a great Internet site that will help you with your research.

Give it a try! Type http://www.myreportlinks.com into your browser, click on the series title and enter the password, then click on the book title, and scroll down to the Report Links listed for this book.

The Report Links will bring you to great source documents, photographs, and illustrations. MyReportLinks.com Books save you time, feature Report Links that are kept up to date, and make report writing easier than ever! A complete listing of the Report Links can be found on pages 116–117 at the back of the book.

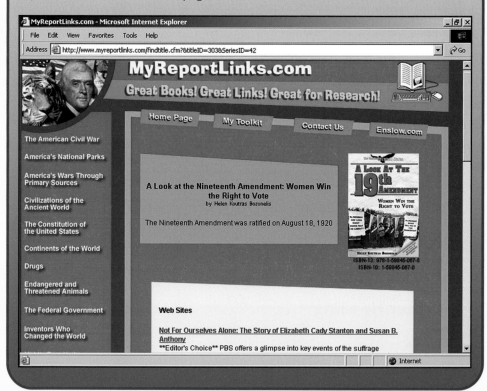

Please see "To Our Readers" on the copyright page for important information about this book, the MyReportLinks.com Web site, and the Report Links that back up this book.

Please enter NAC1822 if asked for a password.

TIME LINE

1848 — The first Women's Rights Convention is held in Seneca Falls, New York.

1861 –1865 — Suffragists suspend their campaign during the Civil War and help the war effort.

1865 — The Thirteenth Amendment abolishing slavery is passed.

1866 — Elizabeth Cady Stanton and Susan B. Anthony form the American Equal Rights Association (AERA) for African Americans and women.

1868 — The Fourteenth Amendment guaranteeing equal protection to African-American men is adopted.

1869 — George Julian introduces an amendment for women's suffrage into Congress.

1870 — The Fifteenth Amendment guarantees voting rights to all males.

1872 — Susan B. Anthony is arrested for trying to vote. She is found guilty seven months later.

1874 — In the case of *Minor v. Happersett,* the U.S. Supreme Court rules that women are citizens, but not voters.

1878 — The Anthony Amendment for women's suffrage is introduced into Congress. It is defeated.

1887 — The U.S. Senate votes for the first time on the national women's suffrage amendment and defeats it, 34 to 16.

1890 — National American Woman Suffrage Association (NAWSA) is formed and begins a state-by-state campaign for a national amendment.

— Wyoming becomes the first state to grant voting rights to women.

1913 — Illinois becomes the first state east of the Mississippi to allow women to vote in presidential elections.

1914 — For the second time, the U.S. Senate defeats the women's suffrage amendment, 35 to 34.

1915 — The U.S. House votes for the first time on the national women's suffrage amendment and defeats it, 204 to 174.

1917 —Women from the National Woman's Party picket in front of the White House, demanding suffrage.

—Pickets are arrested outside the White House for the first time.

1918 —President Wilson announces support for the amendment on women's suffrage.

—The U.S. House passes the women's suffrage amendment by two thirds, 274 to 136.

—The U.S. Senate defeats the women's suffrage amendment for the third time, 62 to 34.

1919 —The U.S. Senate defeats the women's suffrage amendment for the fourth time, 63 to 33.

—The U.S. House passes the suffrage amendment, 304 to 89.

—The U.S. Senate finally passes the amendment, 66 to 30.

—The Nineteenth Amendment to the Constitution granting suffrage to women is adopted by joint resolution of Congress and sent to the states for ratification.

1920 —Tennessee becomes the thirty-sixth and final state needed to ratify the Susan B. Anthony amendment.

—The Nineteenth Amendment becomes part of the United States Constitution.

—Women go to the polls to vote in a presidential election for the first time.

1922 —United States Supreme Court decides *Leser v. Garnett,* holding that the Nineteenth Amendment has been constitutionally established.

1923 —The Equal Rights Amendment, as drafted by Alice Paul, is introduced into Congress.

1963 —Congress passes legislation guaranteeing women equal pay for equal work.

1966 —The National Organization for Women is founded.

1972 —Both houses of Congress pass the Equal Rights Amendment. The amendment fell three states short of ratification. It expired in 1982.

1981 —Sandra Day O'Connor becomes the first woman associate justice to serve on the U.S. Supreme Court.

THEY SUFFERED FOR SUFFRAGE

1

It was a dark, cold November evening in 1917. The attack came out of nowhere. The women were not expecting it. They sat together in this large pit of a room, called the reception area.

At about seven o'clock, the warden, a rough man named Raymond Whittaker, burst into the room "like a tornado," said one of the women.

When Dora Lewis opened her mouth to speak, Whittaker grabbed her by the back of her neck. "You shut up," he yelled. "I have men here to handle you." Then he shouted to his guards, "Seize her!"[1]

Whittaker ordered his guards to teach the prisoners a lesson. "Instantly the room was in havoc. The guards brought from the male prison fell upon us. . . . The furniture was overturned, and the room was a scene of havoc," one woman reported.[2] Forty prison guards beat and choked the thirty-three women and shoved them into cells.

The guards were particularly rough with Lucy Burns. They thought she was a troublemaker. She resisted and was severely beaten. She was thrown into a cell and the guards chained her hands high above her head and let her hang overnight. Bleeding and gasping for air, she tried to call out to the other women. The guards threatened to put her in a straitjacket.

Mrs. Mary Nolan, the oldest, was seventy-three years old and handicapped. She said:

> A man sprang at me and caught me by the shoulder. I remember saying, "I'll come with you; don't drag me; I have a lame foot." But I was jerked down the steps and away into the dark. . . .

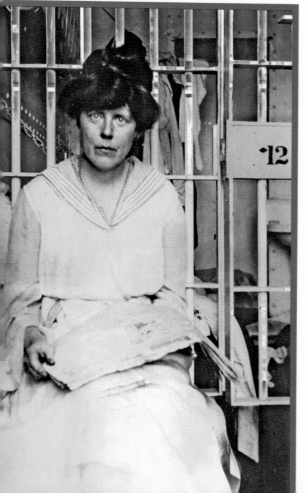

> . . .We were rushed into a large room that opened on a large hall with stone cells on each side. They were perfectly dark. Punishment cells is what they call them. Mine was filthy. It had no window save a slip at the top and no furniture but an iron bed covered with a thin straw pad, and an open toilet flushed from outside the cell. . . .[3]

◀ Lucy Burns, shown here in front of a prison cell, probably at Occoquan Workhouse in Virginia, spent more time in jail than any other woman in the suffrage movement.

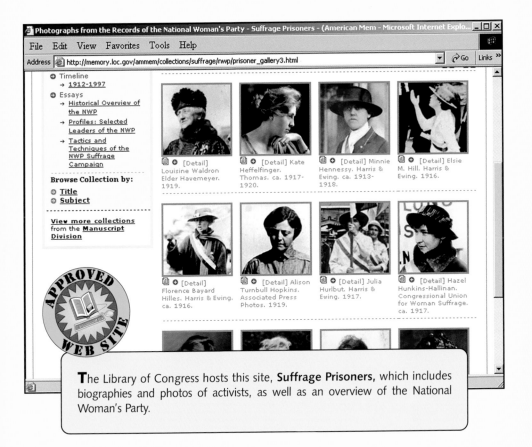

File   Edit   View   Favorites   Tools   Help

Address http://memory.loc.gov/ammem/collections/suffrage/nwp/prisoner_gallery3.html

Photographs from the Records of the National Woman's Party - Suffrage Prisoners - (American Mem - Microsoft Internet Explo...

○ Timeline
→ 1912-1997
○ Essays
→ Historical Overview of the NWP
→ Profiles: Selected Leaders of the NWP
→ Tactics and Techniques of the NWP Suffrage Campaign

Browse Collection by:
○ Title
○ Subject

View more collections from the Manuscript Division

[Detail] Louisine Waldron Elder Havemeyer. 1919.

[Detail] Kate Heffelfinger. Thomas. ca. 1917-1920.

[Detail] Minnie Hennessy. Harris & Ewing. ca. 1913-1918.

[Detail] Elsie M. Hill. Harris & Ewing. 1916.

[Detail] Florence Bayard Hilles. Harris & Ewing. ca. 1916.

[Detail] Alison Turnbull Hopkins. Associated Press Photos. 1919.

[Detail] Julia Hurlbut. Harris & Ewing. 1917.

[Detail] Hazel Hunkins-Hallinan. Congressional Union for Woman Suffrage. ca. 1917.

The Library of Congress hosts this site, **Suffrage Prisoners,** which includes biographies and photos of activists, as well as an overview of the National Woman's Party.

There were more horror stories. When the women cried, Whittaker came to the door and terrorized them, warning them to be quiet. If they were not, he threatened to put them in straight-jackets.

The guards' angry rampage continued.

Gladys Greiner was assaulted for opening a window. Julia Emory was thrown against a wall and choked when she tried to get a drink of water. Dora Lewis was knocked out when her head was smashed against an iron bed.

Cora Week said, "[A]s I was sitting in a chair quietly reading a paper two rough guards rushed into the room from the dark night outside, fell upon me from the rear, seized my arms, bending them sharply backward, dragging me backward over the chairtops and suitcases and so out into the darkness."[4]

Mrs. Mary Butterworth, a civic leader from New York, was ". . . placed in a part of the jail where there were only men. They told her that she was alone with the men, and that they could do what they pleased with her," reported another woman.[5]

Two guards grabbed Dorothy Day, who was the founder of a Catholic workers group, and twisted her arms above her head. ". . . They lifted her, brought her body down twice over the back of an iron bench . . . bruising her back and shoulders. One guard's hand was at her throat to choke her." No one treated her injuries. A guard yelled, "The damned Suffrager! My mother ain't no Suffrager! I will put you through hell!"[6]

Why were these women in jail? What had they done to make the police treat them so savagely? Were they trying to overthrow the government?

⇒Obstructing Sidewalk Traffic

These women had been convicted of "obstructing sidewalk traffic," which was, in fact, a phony charge. They had been arrested outside the White

House on November 13, 1917—they had dared carry banners asking the president to grant women the right to vote, called suffrage. This basic right was denied to American women. These prisoners, known as suffragists, had worked long and hard to win women the right to vote.

The next day, the *Washington Post* reported that the women carried banners

> . . . and paraded unmolested before the gates of the White House for some time. As the crowds poured from the Government departments and packed the street, boys set upon the women and

Supporters of women's suffrage protest the policies of President Woodrow Wilson on the streets of Chicago in this photo taken in 1916.

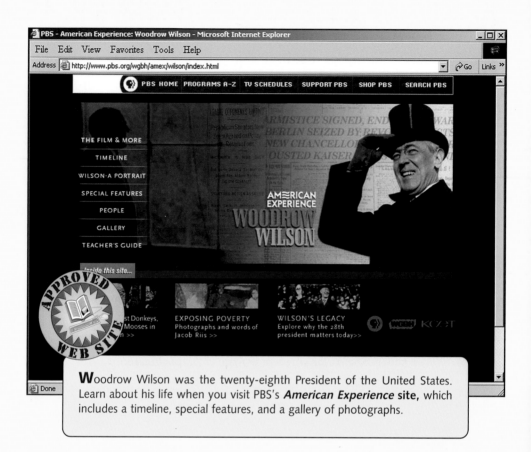

PBS - American Experience: Woodrow Wilson - Microsoft Internet Explorer

File Edit View Favorites Tools Help

Address http://www.pbs.org/wgbh/amex/wilson/index.html

PBS HOME   PROGRAMS A-Z   TV SCHEDULES   SUPPORT PBS   SHOP PBS   SEARCH PBS

THE FILM & MORE

TIMELINE

WILSON-A PORTRAIT

SPECIAL FEATURES

PEOPLE

GALLERY

TEACHER'S GUIDE

Inside this site...

EXPOSING POVERTY
Photographs and words of
Jacob Riis >>

WILSON'S LEGACY
Explore why the 28th
president matters today>>

Woodrow Wilson was the twenty-eighth President of the United States. Learn about his life when you visit PBS's *American Experience* site, which includes a timeline, special features, and a gallery of photographs.

tore down their banners. Some of the women in defending themselves were roughly handled. When the police arrived the disorder had subsided. They arrested the women and took them in patrol wagons to the House of Detention, where they were locked up. . . . Suffrage leaders demanded of the police that they arrest the boys who had attacked, but the police said they were unable to find anybody who had torn down the banners.[7]

The women refused to pay any fines and were sent to jail. Among those punished were a school teacher, a physician, a nurse, a writer, an artist, and the daughter of a former ambassador to Great Britain. These women came together from all areas of society to fight for the right of American women to vote. They were not the first women to be arrested, nor would they be the last.

These women had been warned to stop protesting in front of the White House. Whittaker, the warden at Occoquan Workhouse in Virginia where they were locked up, had threatened to stop them even if some women died in the process. Ironically, at the same time these women were fighting for what they considered their rights, President Woodrow Wilson, who did not support the right of women to vote, was sending American troops to Europe to fight for democracy in World War I.

➔ NIGHT OF TERROR

This violence was designed to scare the women into stopping their protest.[8] The suffragists had to be taught a lesson about criticizing the government during war. The campaign of terror began as soon as the women arrived at Occoquan. The guards enjoyed their role. November 14, 1917, a night of violence and abuse of power, came to be called the "Night of Terror." It was a dark moment in American history.

These women endured life-threatening torture during their confinement at the prison. Some barely survived. But while the guards may have broken their bodies, they could not break the

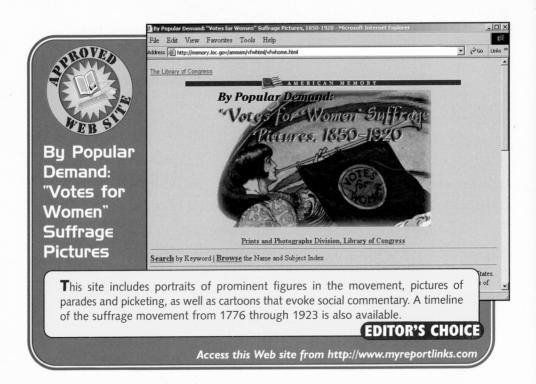

By Popular Demand: "Votes for Women" Suffrage Pictures

By Popular Demand:
"Votes for Women" Suffrage Pictures, 1850-1920 - Microsoft Internet Explorer

File   Edit   View   Favorites   Tools   Help

Address http://memory.loc.gov/ammem/vfwhtml/vfwhome.html   Go   Links »

The Library of Congress

AMERICAN MEMORY

By Popular Demand:
"Votes for Women" Suffrage Pictures, 1850-1920

Prints and Photographs Division, Library of Congress

Search by Keyword | Browse the Name and Subject Index

This site includes portraits of prominent figures in the movement, pictures of parades and picketing, as well as cartoons that evoke social commentary. A timeline of the suffrage movement from 1776 through 1923 is also available.

EDITOR'S CHOICE

Access this Web site from http://www.myreportlinks.com

women's spirit—these incredible women simply refused to stop fighting for what they believed in.

This is the story of their long, difficult struggle to win the right to vote. It is the story of the women who suffered for suffrage, the story of the passage of the Nineteenth Amendment to the U.S. Constitution.

"FAILURE IS IMPOSSIBLE"

2

hen the Founding Fathers wrote the Constitution, they ignored their wives, their mothers, their sisters, and their daughters. The government of the United States was created by men and for men—the word "woman" does not appear anywhere in the text of the Constitution. In Article I, Section 2, they wrote about "Indians" and they even determined that slaves were equal to "three fifths" of a white person. The men who wrote "Liberty and justice for all," did not think it was necessary to mention women.

The right to vote is a basic principle of our government. However, the Constitution of 1787 does not expressly provide the right to vote to any citizen.[1] There are two Articles that together amount to such a right. Article I, Section 2, paragraph 1 gives the right to vote for members of the House of Representatives to those "who have the Qualifications requisite for Electors of the most numerous Branch of the State legislature." Article IV, Section 4, states "The United States shall

15

guarantee to every State in this Union a Republican Form of Government."

Who was allowed to vote under the Constitution? Virtually all white male adults who owned property. Over the years, the right to vote has been expanded to include a broader class of citizens. In fact, there are more constitutional amendments concerning the right to vote than there are relating to any other issue.[2] But it wasn't until 1920, or one hundred thirty years after the Constitution was ratified, that women were given the same right as men—to vote on election day. The nation

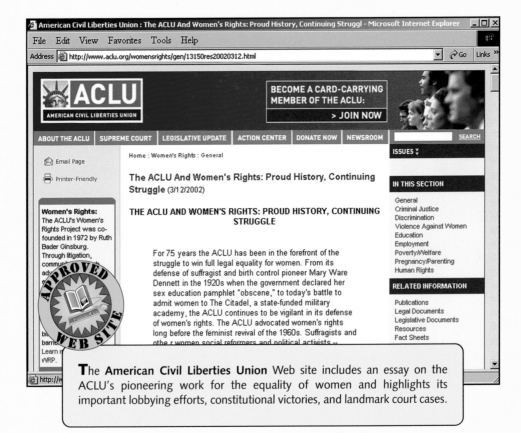

The **American Civil Liberties Union** Web site includes an essay on the ACLU's pioneering work for the equality of women and highlights its important lobbying efforts, constitutional victories, and landmark court cases.

that prided itself as the greatest democracy in the world denied half its citizens the right to vote.

⮕ A Woman's Place

From the beginning, the laws of the United States held women to be inferior to men. This was a democracy of, by, and for white men. In fact, the Constitution did not give women *any* rights. Women, especially married women, were thought to be inferior. And while common law did give single women some of the same rights as a man, it was done for a very offensive reason: It was believed that a single woman needed to be protected because she did not have a man to care for her. But once a woman married, she was considered the property of her husband and her rights were given up to him.

Women could not own property, inherit money, keep money they earned, or sign a contract. They could not attend college, or be legal guardians of their own children. They could not sit on a jury and could not run for political office. They could not even speak at public meetings. Some state laws allowed husbands to beat their wives "with a reasonable instrument."[3] If a woman's husband died without a will in New York her inheritance was limited to one-third his estate, a Bible, the spinning wheel, ten sheep, two pigs, "one table, six chairs, six knives and forks, six tea-cups and saucers, one sugar dish, one milk-pot and six spoons." Girls

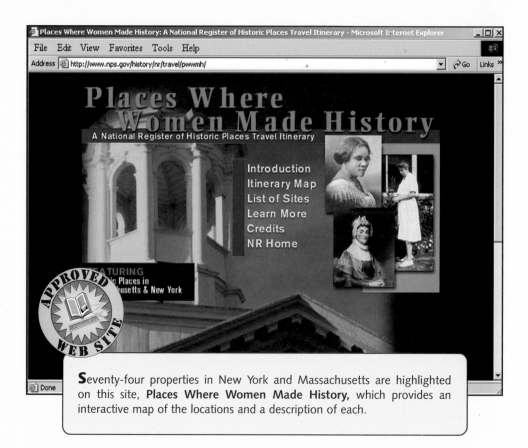

Places Where Women Made History: A National Register of Historic Places Travel Itinerary - Microsoft Internet Explorer

File   Edit   View   Favorites   Tools   Help

Address http://www.nps.gov/history/nr/travel/pwwmh/

Places Where Women Made History

A National Register of Historic Places Travel Itinerary

Introduction
Itinerary Map
List of Sites
Learn More
Credits
NR Home

FEATURING
ic Places in
usetts & New York

APPROVED WEB SITE

Done

Seventy-four properties in New York and Massachusetts are highlighted on this site, **Places Where Women Made History,** which provides an interactive map of the locations and a description of each.

were seldom included in their fathers' wills.[4] A woman's place was in her home, and her life centered on raising children and keeping house.

→ WHAT WOMEN REALLY WANTED

Some women wanted to change their political and legal status. They wanted to become more involved in issues of their day and make changes to improve society. As they became more educated, they became involved in reform movements. They wanted more rights for themselves—especially the right to vote.

Abigail Adams wrote many letters to her husband, John, while he was helping write the Declaration of Independence. She often included her views on public issues. In one letter, Mrs. Adams argued for women's voting rights: "In the new code of laws. . . . remember the ladies. . . . Do not put such unlimited power in the hands of the husbands. Remember, all men would be tyrants if they could. . . ."[5]

While the overwhelming majority of American women couldn't vote until the Nineteenth Amendment was passed in 1920, there were a few states and colonies that allowed women that luxury.

➔ DECLARATION OF SENTIMENTS

The battle to secure the right to vote for women began during the anti-slavery crusade. Women and abolitionists, those who opposed slavery, worked together. They felt the oppression of slaves was similar to the oppression of women. Mary Chestnut, who was married to a slave owner, summed it up in her diary: "[T]here is no slave, after all, like a wife. You know how women sell themselves and are sold in marriage, from queens downward. Poor women, poor slaves."[6]

Two abolitionists, Elizabeth Cady Stanton and Lucretia Mott, were disturbed by the way some men treated women in the abolition movement. Neither Stanton nor Mott was allowed to participate in the World Anti-Slavery Convention in London.

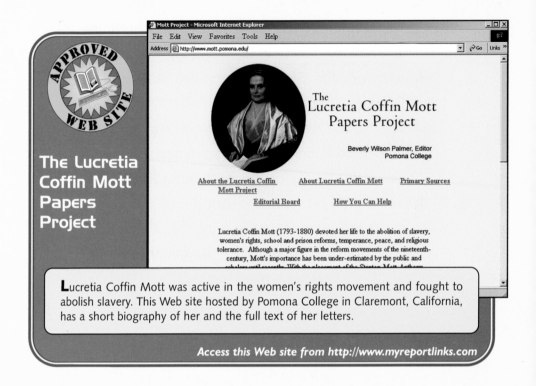

The Lucretia Coffin Mott Papers Project

Lucretia Coffin Mott was active in the women's rights movement and fought to abolish slavery. This Web site hosted by Pomona College in Claremont, California, has a short biography of her and the full text of her letters.

Access this Web site from http://www.myreportlinks.com

They had to sit behind a curtain, hidden from view. So when Stanton and Mott returned to the United States, they decided to act. They and three other women held a public meeting to discuss the lack of rights of American women.

The year 1848 launched the women's rights movement. On July 19 and 20, Stanton and Mott led the first Women's Rights Convention in Seneca Falls, New York. This took great courage—so-called respectable women did not speak in public. Stanton was a thirty-two-year-old mother of three young boys; Mott was a fifty-five-year-old mother of five adult children. Mott had been raised as a Quaker and was a Quaker minister. Her faith taught her that all people were created equal. The first meeting attracted about three hundred women and their male sympathizers. Many abolitionists attended, including a man named Frederick Douglass, who became the star of the convention.

➔ SENECA FALLS

During the two days, the members cleverly rewrote the Declaration of Independence and called it the Declaration of Sentiments and Resolutions. They changed "all men are created equal" to "all men and women are created equal." The attendees called for women to revolt against the "absolute tyranny" of men and listed eighteen complaints about laws that gave men unfair control over women. They outlined twelve issues and goals for women, including better education, better job opportunities, child custody laws—and the right to vote.

Everyone agreed on all the resolutions except one: a woman's right to vote. This idea shocked the audience, some of whom felt that women were already represented by their husbands, fathers, or brothers. Even the leaders argued among themselves. Stanton and Douglass favored it; Mott opposed it. Many women and men were afraid that it was too radical. After a long debate, it passed by a slim margin.

At the end of the convention, one hundred people signed the declaration. The public and the press

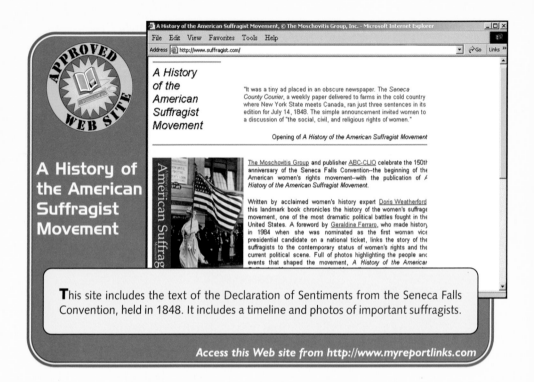

A History
of the
American
Suffragist
Movement

"It was a tiny ad placed in an obscure newspaper. The *Seneca County Courier*, a weekly paper delivered to farms in the cold country where New York State meets Canada, ran just three sentences in its edition for July 14, 1848. The simple announcement invited women to a discussion of "the social, civil, and religious rights of women."

Opening of *A History of the American Suffragist Movement*

A History of the American Suffragist Movement

The Moschovitis Group and publisher ABC-CLIO celebrate the 150th anniversary of the Seneca Falls Convention—the beginning of the American women's rights movement—with the publication of *A History of the American Suffragist Movement*.

Written by acclaimed women's history expert Doris Weatherford this landmark book chronicles the history of the women's suffrage movement, one of the most dramatic political battles fought in the United States. A foreword by Geraldine Ferraro, who made history in 1984 when she was nominated as the first woman vice presidential candidate on a national ticket, links the story of the suffragists to the contemporary status of women's rights and the current political scene. Full of photos highlighting the people and events that shaped the movement, *A History of the American*

This site includes the text of the Declaration of Sentiments from the Seneca Falls Convention, held in 1848. It includes a timeline and photos of important suffragists.

Access this Web site from http://www.myreportlinks.com

ridiculed their efforts. But, for the next seventy years, the issue of women's suffrage remained the primary goal. Leaders believed that if women could vote, they would use that power to achieve equality in other areas. Seneca Falls thrust the issue of women's suffrage into the national spotlight.

➔FOUNDING SISTERS

After the Seneca Falls convention, more women joined the struggle. One, Susan B. Anthony, had been a schoolteacher and was active in the movement to pass laws that would ban the production and sale of liquor. She was an independent thinker and an imposing figure.

Anthony and Elizabeth Cady Stanton met and forged a special friendship that lasted fifty years. These two women were opposites in lifestyle, personality, and almost every other manner possible; but somehow, they complemented each other. Together, they became the prominent leaders and the driving force of the women's rights movement. Of their relationship, Stanton once wrote: "I am the better writer, she the better critic. . . . and together we have made arguments that have stood unshaken by the storms of . . . long years; arguments that no man has answered."[7]

Before the Civil War, which began in 1861 and ended in 1865, these pioneers and others worked hard to win the right to vote for women. They traveled around the country making speeches, lecturing, writing letters and publishing articles. Some petitioned their state legislatures to change laws that were unfair to women.

➲ NATION AT WAR

The Civil War was a terrible crisis that threatened to destroy the United States. When it began, Stanton and Anthony had a disagreement. Stanton wanted to suspend the campaign for women's rights and refocus their energy on the war; she thought it was the loyal and moral thing to do. She argued this would be an opportunity for women to demonstrate their patriotism and highlight their

Elizabeth Cady Stanton (seated) and Susan B. Anthony met soon after the Seneca Falls convention in 1848; the two were the heart and soul of the early suffrage movement.

contributions to society for which they would be rewarded with the vote.

Anthony flatly disagreed. She was afraid that the little progress they had slowly and painfully gained until then would be lost. She believed women had to continue to fight. Anthony reluctantly gave in. Women from the North and the South threw themselves into the war effort. Thousands served as nurses and hundreds disguised themselves as men and went off to fight. Some learned new trades while others managed the family farms or businesses left behind by their husbands and fathers.

"THE NEGRO'S HOUR"

In 1866, Stanton joined forces with Lucy Stone, another outspoken pioneer for suffrage and other women's rights (Stone was the first woman to keep her maiden name after marriage, a radical move at the time). They formed the American

Equal Rights Association (AERA), also called the Equal Rights Association, which combined the abolition and suffrage movements. Its goal was universal suffrage—that is, give all adults the right to vote, regardless of race or sex.

When the Civil War ended, Congress began work on amendments that would outlaw slavery and allow African-American men to vote. Congress passed three amendments to the Constitution. The Thirteenth Amendment, which passed in 1865, abolished slavery. The Fourteenth Amendment (1868), gave the vote to all adult "male" citizens over the age of twenty-one. It was intended to give the vote to former slaves (and it marks the first time

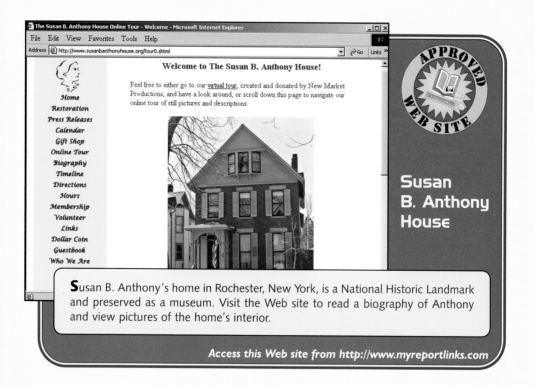

Susan B. Anthony's home in Rochester, New York, is a National Historic Landmark and preserved as a museum. Visit the Web site to read a biography of Anthony and view pictures of the home's interior.

Access this Web site from http://www.myreportlinks.com

25

the word *male* was used in the Constitution). The Fourteenth Amendment has two important clauses—the due process of law clause says that no one can be deprived of life, liberty, or property without legal procedures; and the equal protection clause, which gives equal protection of the law to all citizens. The Fifteenth Amendment (1870) gave African-American men the right to vote—but not women, black or white. They remained legally inferior to men. Stanton and Anthony were told this is the "Negro's hour."·

Stanton and Anthony felt betrayed. They objected to the wording of the Fourteenth and Fifteenth amendments which contained the phrase "male citizen." They worked tirelessly to have the

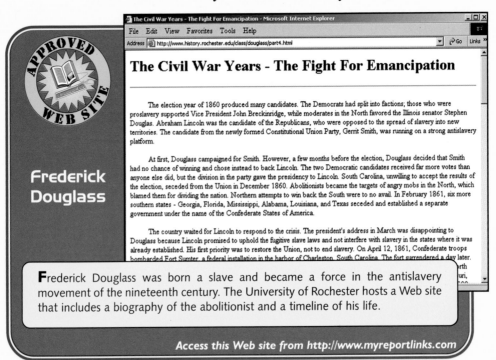

Frederick Douglass

The Civil War Years - The Fight For Emancipation

The election year of 1860 produced many candidates. The Democrats had split into factions; those who were proslavery supported Vice President John Breckinridge, while moderates in the North favored the Illinois senator Stephen Douglas. Abraham Lincoln was the candidate of the Republicans, who were opposed to the spread of slavery into new territories. The candidate from the newly formed Constitutional Union Party, Gerrit Smith, was running on a strong antislavery platform.

At first, Douglass campaigned for Smith. However, a few months before the election, Douglass decided that Smith had no chance of winning and chose instead to back Lincoln. The two Democratic candidates received far more votes than anyone else did, but the division in the party gave the presidency to Lincoln. South Carolina, unwilling to accept the results of the election, seceded from the Union in December 1860. Abolitionists became the targets of angry mobs in the North, which blamed them for dividing the nation. Northern attempts to win back the South were to no avail. In February 1861, six more southern states - Georgia, Florida, Mississippi, Alabama, Louisiana, and Texas seceded and established a separate government under the name of the Confederate States of America.

The country waited for Lincoln to respond to the crisis. The president's address in March was disappointing to Douglass because Lincoln promised to uphold the fugitive slave laws and not interfere with slavery in the states where it was already established. His first priority was to restore the Union, not to end slavery. On April 12, 1861, Confederate troops bombarded Fort Sumter, a federal installation in the harbor of Charleston, South Carolina. The fort surrendered a day later.

Frederick Douglass was born a slave and became a force in the antislavery movement of the nineteenth century. The University of Rochester hosts a Web site that includes a biography of the abolitionist and a timeline of his life.

Access this Web site from http://www.myreportlinks.com

Amendment reworded, but failed. They accused abolitionists of concentrating on African American civil rights at the expense of women's rights. Stanton asked, "Do you believe the African race is composed entirely of males?"[8] Anthony declared: "I will cut off this right arm of mine before I will work for or demand the ballot for the Negro and not the woman."[9] Their reaction showed underlying feelings of racism, even though they had worked for abolition.

But Frederick Douglass didn't understand Stanton or Anthony's frustration. "I must say that I do not see how any one can pretend that there is the same urgency in giving the ballot to women as to the negro," he said at the 1869 meeting of the American Equal Rights Association. "With us, the matter is a question of life and death. . . . When women, because they are women, are hunted down through the cities of New York and New Orleans; when they are dragged from their houses and hung upon lamp-posts . . . then they will have an urgency to obtain the ballot equal to our own."[10]

→ WOMEN, IDIOTS, FELONS AND LUNATICS

The women's movement split in two in 1869. In May, Stanton and Anthony formed a new political group, the National Woman's Suffrage Association (NWSA). This group demanded sweeping changes to improve the status of women and used

Sojourner Truth, shown in this 1864 photograph, was a former slave who could not read or write. Still, she became famous for her wonderful and eloquent speeches in support of women's suffrage.

radical tactics to achieve that end. The NWSA did not allow men into its membership. It focused on campaigning at the national level for another constitutional amendment to guarantee women's voting rights. Even the group's newspaper, named *The Revolution,* announced their radicalism.

Six months later, Lucy Stone founded a rival group, the American Woman's Suffrage Association (AWSA) which was more conservative and worked to secure the vote for women through smaller, state-by-state campaigns. Stone's group named its newspaper *Women's Journal.* AWSA protested the methods of NWSA.

In 1869, Stone wrote "An Appeal to the Men and Women of America":

> Get every man or woman to sign [this petition] who is not satisfied while women, idiots, felons, and lunatics are the only classes excluded from the

exercise of the right of suffrage. Let the great army of working-women, who wish to secure a fair day's wages for a fair day's work, Sign It. Let the wife, from whom the law takes the right to what she earns, Sign It. Let the mother, who has no legal right to her own children, Sign It. . . . .[11]

→ JUST TWENTY-TWO WORDS

In 1872, women of the radical wing brought a series of court challenges to test whether voting was a privilege granted by the U.S. Constitution. They claimed they were allowed to vote under the recently adopted Fourteenth Amendment. Hundreds of women went to vote. Susan B. Anthony was arrested and put on trial because she dared vote.

In 1878, this same group introduced the first Woman Suffrage Amendment into Congress. It said: "The right of citizens to vote shall not be abridged by the United States or by any State on account of sex." Just twenty-two words. It was defeated. It would not make it to the floor of Congress for a vote until 1887. Each year for the next forty-one years, suffragists would introduce this same amendment into every session of Congress.

For the next twenty-one years, the AWSA and NWSA campaigned separately. Members of both groups toured the country, gave speeches, handed out pamphlets, and tried to drum up support for women's suffrage. Neither group had much success.

→ THE ICE IS CRACKED

After the Civil War, newly free African-American women faced enormous struggles. They found themselves torn between loyalty to their race or to their gender. And they felt their status had not changed. Their former masters still considered these women and their children to be their property. As one former slaveholder said, "I acknowledge her freedom, but I do not acknowledge her right to do as she wishes."[12]

The first known African-American suffragist was Sojourner Truth, a former slave. She could not read or write, but she became famous for her speeches. In May 1867, Truth was invited to address the first meeting of the American Equal Rights Association. She won the audience with her eloquence:

> My friends. . . There is a great stir about colored men getting their rights, but not a word about the colored women; and if colored men get their rights, and not colored women theirs, you see the colored men will be masters over the women, and it will be just as bad as it was before. . . . I want women to have their rights. In the courts women have no right, no voice; nobody speaks for them. . . . I want to keep the thing stirring now that the ice is cracked. . . . [W]hen we have got this battle once fought we shall not be coming to you any more. You have been having our rights so long, that you think, like a slave-holder, that you own us. I know

that it is hard for one who has held the reins for so long to give up; it cuts like a knife. . . . Now colored men have the right to vote. There ought to be equal rights now more than ever. . . .[13]

⮕ BLACK AND WHITE

Mary Church Terrell, born in 1863, was another prominent African-American suffragist. Her parents had been slaves, but through hard work, became wealthy. Mary went to college and became one of the first African-American women to earn a college degree. She was a member of the National American Women Suffrage Association which was one of just a few national organizations that admitted African-American women. She tried to bring up issues of racial equality, but NAWSA felt it was the "woman's hour" and kept its focus on voting rights for all women. Some black women became frustrated with the white suffragists; in 1896, Terrell helped form the National Association of Colored Women (NACW) and became its first president.

Terrell was a popular speaker at women's suffrage conventions. In a speech before NAWSA in 1898, she spoke about the discrimination that African-American women felt. "For, not only are colored women with ambition and aspiration handicapped on account of their sex," she said, "but they are everywhere baffled and mocked on account of their race. . . . Avocations opened and opportunities offered to their more favored [white] sisters have been and are tonight closed and barred against them."[14]

→NOT WITHOUT OUR WOMEN

By the late 1860s, the booming West provided women's suffrage with opportunities the conservative eastern states did not. Men wanted women to move west and help settle the sparsely populated areas. To encourage them, some territories granted women the right to vote in local elections.

In 1869, Wyoming became the first territory to give women the right to vote. Indeed, when Wyoming Territory applied to become a state in

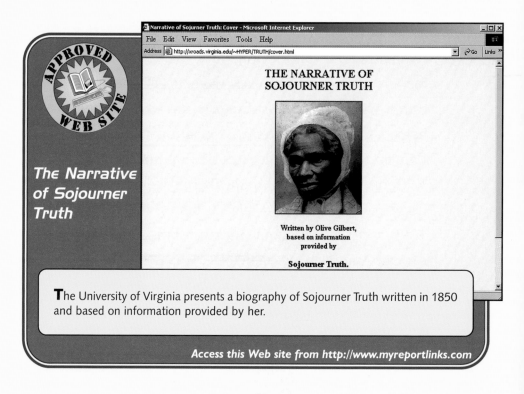

The Narrative of Sojourner Truth

THE NARRATIVE OF SOJOURNER TRUTH

Written by Olive Gilbert, based on information provided by

Sojourner Truth.

The University of Virginia presents a biography of Sojourner Truth written in 1850 and based on information provided by her.

Access this Web site from http://www.myreportlinks.com

1889, some U.S. congressmen were opposed because Wyoming let women vote. William C. Oates complained, "I like a woman who is a woman and appreciates the sphere to which God and the Bible have assigned her. I do not like a man-woman."[15] But the people of Wyoming refused to give in. Their legislature wired this answer back to Washington, D.C.: "We will remain out of the Union a hundred years rather than come in without our women!"[16] The West won. And Wyoming became the first and only suffrage state in the Union.

Over the next forty-five years, only ten additional states followed suit.

⇨ THE ANTIS

In a book published in 1884, Francis Parkman gave reasons why women should not be allowed to vote: "Because they cannot do their own work . . . unhappy marriages will be multiplied and divorces redoubled. . . . The female vote would enormously increase the evil . . . less subject to reason . . . woman suffragists have done nothing to prove their fitness for a share in government. . . ."[17]

But men were not the only ones who did not want women to vote. Many women were fiercely opposed to giving themselves this right. These women were known as antisuffragists, or "antis." For the most part, these women lived in the eastern states and were wealthy and well-educated. They

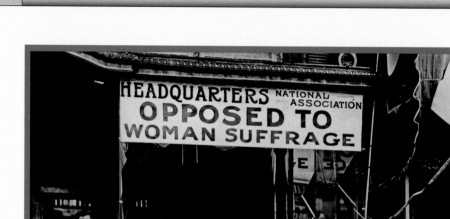

▲ Many men—and some women, too—were extremely opposed to the idea of giving women the vote; and like the women of the suffrage movement, anti-suffragists worked hard to convince the public that their cause was just.

had great political influence through the social service groups they led.

The first anti-suffrage group formed in 1871 in Washington, D.C. By 1911, a larger, more visible group formed, called the National Association Opposed to Woman Suffrage. The antis dismissed suffragists as women who had no home or family life. They believed that if married women could vote, there would be more divorces and child neglect. But, simmering below the surface, there was another reason why the antis opposed suffrage: They wanted to keep the vote from women they considered "inferior" in order to protect their interests and maintain their higher status in society.[18]

➔ UGLY RACISM

Even after the Civil War, southern states did not want African Americans to vote, especially African-American women. Some states made African-American men pass literacy tests to prove they could read or write. Needless to say, since most former slaves had never been taught, they could not vote. Some states passed a poll tax, basically a fee that a person had to pay in order to vote. Most former slaves were poor and they could not pay, so they could not vote. Then, there was the grandfather clause, an especially nasty rule that stated that a person could vote—*if* his grandfather had voted. The grandfathers of most slaves were slaves themselves, therefore voting was impossible.

These rules were designed to prevent African Americans—men and women—from voting. And as difficult as it would be for women to win the right to vote, these would prove to be even greater obstacles for African-American women to overcome.

➔ TOGETHER AGAIN

By 1890, the two rival groups, the National Women's Suffrage Association and the America Women's Suffrage Association merged under a new name: the National American Woman Suffrage Association (NAWSA). Elizabeth Stanton became its president and Susan Anthony became vice president. The unified group took a more moderate approach in its effort to secure the vote for women, creating a constitutional amendment and campaigning state by state. It backed away from other equality issues for women.

→ THE END OF AN ERA

At the turn of the century, the suffrage movement went into a period that its own leaders called "the doldrums." NAWSA, now led by the conservative Dr. Anna Shaw, almost came to a standstill. No progress had been made and no other states passed laws allowing women to vote.

It had been decades since that first meeting at Seneca Falls in 1848 and the first generation of suffragists realized they would not live long enough to cast ballots themselves. Shortly before she died in 1902, Stanton wrote to President Theodore Roosevelt: "Mr. President, Abraham Lincoln immortalized himself by the emancipation of four million slaves. Immortalize yourself by bringing about the complete emancipation of thirty-six million women."[19]

In February 1906, at a celebration for her 86th birthday in Washington, D.C., Anthony gave her last speech. "There have been others also just as true and devoted to the cause," she said. "I wish I could name every one—but with such women consecrating their lives, failure is impossible."[20] She died one month later. The suffrage movement had come to the end of an era.

→ A New Century

The late nineteenth and early twentieth century was a period of great social change in America. The Progressive Era, as it came to be called, was characterized by a desire to improve life for everyone. Indeed, the push for women's rights gained a new momentum.

By this time, more than three million women had jobs outside their homes. Many worked in dangerous conditions. They needed a voice now more than ever. Millions demanded the vote and many wanted to enter public life.

Harriot Stanton Blatch, Elizabeth Cady Stanton's youngest daughter, rose to this challenge. Blatch, who grew up with the women's movement, was one of many suffragists who returned from England where women were also battling for the right to vote. But in London, women were using controversial tactics to raise public awareness. Blatch learned first-hand how to stage protests, organize parades and hunger strikes and other activities that could make news. When she returned to the United States, she took over where her mother had left off.

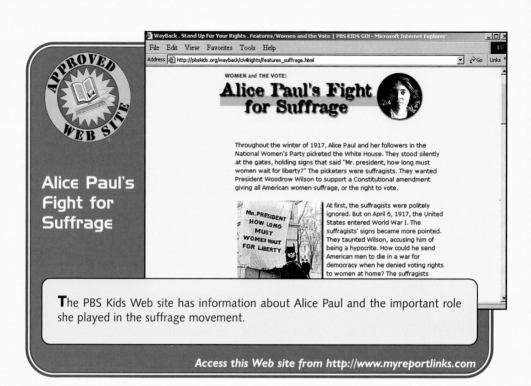

WayBack . Stand Up For Your Rights . Features/Women and the Vote | PBS KIDS GO! - Microsoft Internet Explorer

File   Edit   View   Favorites   Tools   Help

Address http://pbskids.org/wayback/civilrights/features_suffrage.html   Go   Links

WOMEN and THE VOTE:

Alice Paul's Fight for Suffrage

Throughout the winter of 1917, Alice Paul and her followers in the National Women's Party picketed the White House. They stood silently at the gates, holding signs that said "Mr. president, how long must women wait for liberty?" The picketers were suffragists. They wanted President Woodrow Wilson to support a Constitutional amendment giving all American women suffrage, or the right to vote.

At first, the suffragists were politely ignored. But on April 6, 1917, the United States entered World War I. The suffragists' signs became more pointed. They taunted Wilson, accusing him of being a hypocrite. How could he send American men to die in a war for democracy when he denied voting rights to women at home? The suffragists

Alice Paul's Fight for Suffrage

The PBS Kids Web site has information about Alice Paul and the important role she played in the suffrage movement.

Access this Web site from http://www.myreportlinks.com

In 1907, Blatch formed the Equality League of Self-Supporting Women, which later became the Women's Political Union in New York, to influence local lawmakers. She staged annual parades in New York City, where hundreds of women, mostly working women, marched down Fifth Avenue. They wore yellow sashes that read "Votes for Women" and they carried yellow banners. Cheered by some and booed by others, the parades received immediate newspaper coverage.

A WINNING PLAN

Carrie Chapman Catt was hand-picked by Susan B. Anthony to be president of NAWSA, which she led for four years. After the era of "doldrums," Catt was made president again to energize the movement. A dynamic leader, Catt came up with a two-point "Winning Plan." Her goal was to give women the vote in at least thirty-six states, the number needed to ratify a Constitutional amendment. She organized a series of campaigns in each state. She also wanted to try to convince President Wilson that an amendment was needed.

ANOTHER ODD COUPLE

Like Harriot Stanton Blatch, Alice Paul and Lucy Burns had spent time in London and got swept up in the movement and the radical tactics of the British suffragists. They actually met at a London police station after each had been arrested outside Parliament during a demonstration. Both had been arrested several times there. They became fast friends and a dynamic duo. With grit and determination, they would use civil disobedience to further the cause of women's suffrage in America.

Alice Paul was thirty-two years old. Born in New Jersey, she was the daughter of Quaker parents. She was well educated, having earned a doctorate in economics from the University of Pennsylvania. Lucy Burns was thirty-eight years old. She was born in Brooklyn, New York, into an Irish-American family. She did graduate work at Yale University and at Oxford in England. She had

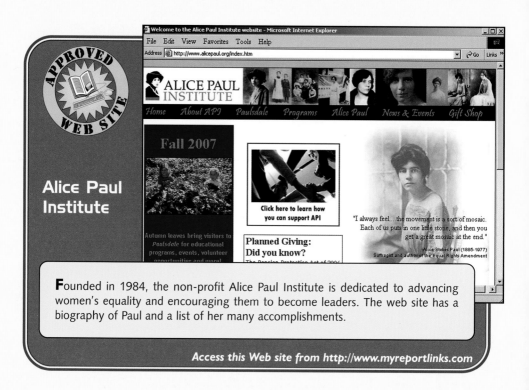

APPROVED WEB SITE

Alice Paul Institute

Welcome to the Alice Paul Institute website - Microsoft Internet Explorer

File   Edit   View   Favorites   Tools   Help

Address http://www.alicepaul.org/index.htm   Go   Links »

ALICE PAUL INSTITUTE

Home   About API   Paulsdale   Programs   Alice Paul   News & Events   Gift Shop

Fall 2007

Click here to learn how you can support API

Planned Giving: Did you know?
The Pension Protection Act of 2006

Autumn leaves bring visitors to Paulsdale for educational programs, events, volunteer opportunities and more!

"I always feel...the movement is a sort of mosaic. Each of us puts in one little stone, and then you get a great mosaic at the end."
(Alice Stokes Paul (1885-1977)
Suffragist and author of the Equal Rights Amendment

Founded in 1984, the non-profit Alice Paul Institute is dedicated to advancing women's equality and encouraging them to become leaders. The web site has a biography of Paul and a list of her many accomplishments.

Access this Web site from http://www.myreportlinks.com

fiery, red hair that people said matched her personality. Burns and Paul knew they needed publicity in order to keep the movement in the public eye.

The women formed the Congressional Union for Woman Suffrage (CU) which became the National Woman's Party (NWP). They had a budget of only thirteen dollars for the year. Their first mission was to upstage the presidential inauguration of Woodrow Wilson.

MARCH ON WASHINGTON

On March 3, 1913, Paul organized a dramatic parade in the heart of Washington, D.C. The parade began at the Capitol, worked its way down Pennsylvania

Avenue, passed the White House, and ended in a rally at the Daughters of the American Revolution Hall. The day before President Wilson's inauguration was perfect.

Inez Milholland led the parade wearing a white gown and riding a white horse. Behind her marched eight thousand supporters. A group of African-American women marched at the back of the parade. Paul, who wanted to keep southern

Official Program WOMAN SUFFRAGE Procession

Washington D.C. March 3, 1913

△ Lucy Burns and Alice Paul helped organize a parade in Washington, D.C., which took place on March 3, 1913, the day before the inauguration of President Woodrow Wilson. Many of those who marched in the parade were attacked by onlookers.

white women happy, forced them to march there. Some southern women were afraid that because there were more black women than white women, black people would become too powerful.[21] Ida B. Wells-Barnett, of Chicago, and Mary Church Terrell were told to go to the back of the parade with other black women. Terrell agreed; Wells-Barnett refused. She waited on a sidewalk until the group from her home state marched by, and then she jumped into line next to them.

As the parade passed, onlookers jeered and became violent. Drunken men shouted obscenities; they tripped and spat on the marchers. The police did not protect the women. More than two hundred people were treated for injuries. The violence made the front page of newspapers all over the country. It was a public relations triumph for women's suffrage.

ANOTHER SPLIT

In 1914, the women's suffrage movement split— the differences between the two main organizations were too great to overcome.

Catt and the National American Woman Suffrage Association adopted a conservative tone, hoping to appeal to mainstream society. NAWSA's two million members emphasized motherhood and social service. They favored winning the vote by campaigning state by state.

WOMAN'S JOURNAL
AND SUFFRAGE NEWS

OL. XLIV. NO. 10   SATURDAY, MARCH 8, 1913   FIVE CENTS

ARADE STRUGGLES TO VICTORY DESPITE DISGRACEFUL SCENES

ation Aroused by Open Insults to Women—Cause Wins Popular Sympathy—Congress Orders Investigation—Striking Object Lesson

Washington has been disgraced. Equal suffrage has scored a great ory. Thousands of indifferent women have been aroused. Influential s are incensed and the United States Senate demands an investigation the treatment given the suffragists at the National Capital on Monday.

'en thousand women from all over country had planned a magnifi- t parade and pageant to take place Washington on March 3. Artists, eant leaders, designers, women of uence and renown were ready to a wonderful and beautiful piece suffrage work to the public that ald throng the National Capital for inauguration festivities. The suf- gists were ready; the whole pro- sion started down Pennsylvania enue, when the police protection, t had been promised, failed them, l a disgraceful scene followed. The wd surged into the space which l been marked off for the paraders, l the leaders of the suffrage move- nt were compelled to push their y through a mob of the worst ele- nt in Washington and vicinity. men were spit upon, slapped in the e, tripped up, pelted with burning ar stubs, and insulted by jeers and scene language too vile to print or eat.

The cause of all the trouble is ap- rent when the facts are known. e police authorities in Washington posed every attempt to have a suf- ge parade at all. Having been for- den a place in the inaugural pro- sion, the suffragists asked to have procession of their own on March They were finally told that they uld have a procession but that it ald not be on Pennsylvania avenue, t must be on a side street. At last y got permission to have the suf- age parade on the avenue, and asked at traffic be excluded from the street ring the parade. For a long time as was denied, and only on Saturday ere they successful.

Everything was at last arranged; it as a glorious day; ten thousand men were ready to do their part to ake the parade beautiful to behold, make it a credit to womanhood and demonstrate the strength of the ovement for their enfranchisement The police were determined, how- er, and they had their way. Their empt to afford the marchers pro- ction and keep the space of the ave- e free for the suffrage procession as the flimsiest sham. Police offi rs stood by with folded arms and inned while the picked women of e land were insulted and roughly used by an ignorant and uncouth ob.

Miss Alice Paul and other suffra- sts were compelled to drive their tomobiles down the avenue to sep- ate the crowds so the suffragists ith the banners and floats could ss. The police officials say their rce was inadequate to handle the owds, but it is noted that there was disorder on the avenue during the augural procession. It is stated that deral troops were offered to the ief of police for the suffrage pro- ession, but that he refused their aid At any rate, assistance was finally lled from Fort Myer and mounted ldiers drove back the crowd so that straggling line of marchers could ss through.

Not only were the suffragists bit rly disappointed in having the effect

(Continued on Page 78)

AMENDMENT WINS IN NEW JERSEY

Easy Victory in Assembly 46 to 5—Equal Suffrage Enthusiasm Runs High

The New Jersey Legislature passed the woman suffrage amend- ment in the Assembly last week by a vote of 46 to 5. The Senate had already voted favorably 14 to 5.

A large delegation of suffragists crowded the galleries, and when the overwhelming vote was announced there was a scene of great enthusi- asm. Women stood in their seats and waved handkerchiefs and "votes for women" flags and cheered them- selves hoarse.

Dr. Jekyll Becomes Mr. Hyde

Opposition was confined exclusive- ly to the old sentimental arguments.

(Continued on Page 79)

MICHIGAN AGAIN CAMPAIGN STATE

Senate Passes Suffrage Amend- ment 26 to 5 and Battle Is Now On

Michigan is again a campaign State after a short lapse of four months. The amendment will go to the voters on April 7. The State-wide feeling that the women were defrauded of victory last fall will help the suf- fragists.

The final action of the Legislature was taken last week, when the Sen- ate, by a vote of 26 to 5, passed the suffrage amendment, with a slight amendment to make the requirements for foreign-born women the same as those for male immigrants.

Governor Watches Debate

The debate in the Senate lasted an hour and a quarter, and was charac- terized by the persistent efforts of Senator Weadock and a few others to tack on crippling amendments. Sev- eral suggestions, including the dis- abling of women for holding office or serving on juries, were voted down in quick succession.

Gov. Ferris was among the visitors who crowded the chamber and gal- lery. Mrs. Clara B. Arthur, Mrs. Thomas R. Henderson and Mrs. Wil- bur Brotherton, of Detroit; Mrs. Jen- nie Law Hardy, of Tecumseh, and other State leaders were present, sup- ported by a large delegation of Lans ing suffragists.

The final stand of the opposition was made by Senator Murtha in the hope of putting off the submission till November, 1914, and this also failed.

Of the five who opposed the meas- ure on the final roll-call, three were from Detroit.

A complete campaign of organiza- tion and education has been mapped out by the State Association. The

(Continued on Page 74.)

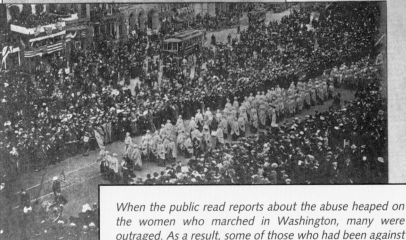

When the public read reports about the abuse heaped on the women who marched in Washington, many were outraged. As a result, some of those who had been against the suffragists began to rethink their opposition.

General Rosalie Jones in Pilgrim Costume; Miss Inez Milholland on White Steed Leading the Parade; One of the Scores of Imposing Floats; One View of the Procession

"I Summon you to Comradeship in the Red Cross"
Woodrow Wilson

During the Civil War, suffragists postponed their efforts to win the vote and, instead, worked to support the war. The movement faced the same dilemma at the outbreak of World War I; once again, some set aside their goals. Shown here, a poster for the Red Cross.

Alice Paul and the National Woman's Party were radical. NWP and its fifty-thousand members wanted an equal rights amendment that would give individual freedom and complete equality under the law to women. They did not have the patience to take the issue to each state. They were determined to jolt Congress to pass a national amendment to the Constitution.

Catt and NAWSA found Paul's aggressive tactics unacceptable, so they distanced themselves from the group.

BREAKING WITH THE PAST

In April 1917, the United States declared war on Germany and entered World War I. Women were again expected to put aside their goal of suffrage and support the war effort—just as they had been asked to do during the Civil War. And once again, suffragists found themselves in a difficult position: In the interest of national unity, should they again shelve debate until after the war?

Harriot Stanton Blatch reminded them: "The suffragists of Civil War days had given up their campaign to work for their country, expecting to be enfranchised in return for all their good services. . . . They were told they must wait. . . . Now in 1917 women [are] still waiting."[22]

Carrie Chapman Catt and other moderates felt that if women appeared patriotic and did not do anything to offend elected officials, they would gain the support needed for a Constitutional amendment. Two million women agreed with Catt and did things like enlist to fight, sell war bonds, and open chapters of the Red Cross.

Not Alice Paul. She knew immediately that she could

By President Woodrow Wilson's second term in office, many suffragists had lost patience at the lack of progress toward an amendment giving them the vote. The National Woman's Party decided to protest outside the White House in an effort to put pressure directly on the president, shown here in a 1917 photo.

not make the same mistake that Elizabeth Cady Stanton made before the Civil War. She and the radical suffragists of the National Woman's Party continued to press President Wilson for the right to vote. How, she wondered, could the United States fight for democracy in Europe, but deny the vote to women at home?

So the suffragists played both sides of the fence, thousands working to support the war effort while thousands worked for the movement.

→THE SILENT SENTINELS

By 1917, Paul and the National Woman's Party had lost patience. They decided to hold President Wilson and his Democratic Party responsible for the lack of progress. To focus attention on the issue, they picketed the White House (picketing is a form of protest in which people gather

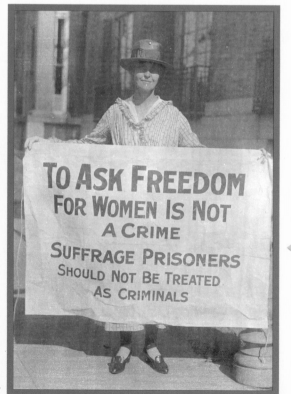

Early protestors were largely ignored by the press and the public. But President Wilson played into the protestors' hands by having many women arrested, which drew attention to their cause. Mary Winsor carries a sign denouncing the arrests.

Frustrated and increasingly angry, suffragists grew more confrontational. Virginia Arnold carries a banner comparing President Wilson to Kaiser Wilhelm, the leader of Germany and the country the United States was fighting in World War I.

outside a public building, often carrying signs, in order to gain public attention).

At 10:00 AM, on January 10, twelve women walked to the White House and formed the first of many picket lines. These women were called the Silent Sentinels because they rarely spoke. Instead they wrote demands on large banners and held them up for the world to see. One banner read: "Mr. President what will you do for woman suffrage?" Another read: "How long must women wait for liberty?" Every day except Sunday, in rain and cold, they kept vigil. Two thousand women picketed over eighteen months.

At first the protesters were well-behaved—and they were ignored. But they became increasingly confrontational, hoping to attract attention and gain support for women's suffrage.

→ JAILED FOR FREEDOM

Much of the country's energy was focused on the war in Europe and, as a result, the radicals seemed unpatriotic. There was little sympathy for their cause. The protesters were heckled. Newspapers did not give them the publicity they wanted and needed.

The first arrests, ordered by President Wilson, came on June 22. Two women were arrested for "obstructing traffic," a fake charge. "We have picketed for six months without interference," said Alice Paul. "Has the law been changed?"[23] They refused to pay fines, but were released anyway.

On June 26, six more pickets were arrested and given a twenty-five dollar fine. They made history that day when they refused to pay the fine and were sent to the District Jail for three days. They were the first suffragists who went to prison for their cause.

Their banners became more demanding. On July 14, French independence day, their banners read "Liberty Equality Fraternity," the motto made famous during the French Revolution in 1848. Police rounded up sixteen more women, including Lucy Burns. (Burns would serve more time in prison than any other suffragist.) Again, the women refused to pay their fines, so they were given a harsh sentence: Sixty days at Occoquan Workhouse in nearby Virginia. Details were leaked to the press about how the women were locked up with common criminals. The public was outraged and the publicity embarrassed President Wilson. He pardoned them after three days.

JAILBIRDS

During the summer, the pickets continued and the violence increased. These women did not regard Wilson as their president. After all, they had not voted for him.[24] On August 14, a banner appeared with a picture of President Wilson looking like Kaiser Wilhelm II, the leader of Germany. It asked the question: "Kaiser Wilson. Have you forgotten how you sympathized with the poor Germans because they were not self-governed? 20,000,000 American women are not self-governed. Take the beam out of your own eye."[25] The mob went wild and attacked the pickets and tore their banners. The police did nothing; some even helped the attackers. After three days, the police arrested several pickets, not the mob; they even arrested men who tried to assist the women.

In September, dozens more women were sent to jail. These "jailbirds," as they were nicknamed, had to spend time either in District Jail in Washington, D.C., or in Occoquan Workhouse. Prison

▲ Of the 500 women arrested picketing the White House, 168 spent time in jail. Above, Kate Heffelfinger is escorted to a car after being released from Occoquan Prison in 1917.

life was harsh: No visitors allowed for the first two weeks, no clean clothes or shoes, buckets instead of toilets; they were forbidden to speak to each other. There were rats everywhere.

Virginia Bovee, a prison matron, reported:

Blankets are washed once a year. . . . The beans, hominy, rice, cornmeal, and cereal have all had worms in them. Sometimes the worms float on top of the soup. Often they are found in the cornbread. The first suffragists sent the worms to Whittaker on a spoon. Prisoners are punished by being put on bread or water, or by being beaten. . . . Superintendent

Whittaker or his son are the only ones who beat the girls. . . .[26]

From 1917 to 1919, five hundred women were arrested, and 168 served jail sentences that ranged from three to six months.[27]

➜ STARVING FOR THE VOTE

On October 20, 1917, Alice Paul was arrested and sentenced to seven months in jail for "obstructing traffic." As she was being taken to prison, she said: "I am being imprisoned not because I obstructed traffic, but because I pointed out to President Wilson

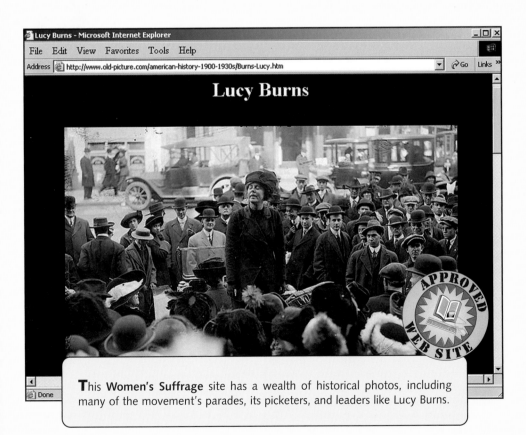

Lucy Burns - Microsoft Internet Explorer

File Edit View Favorites Tools Help

Address http://www.old-picture.com/american-history-1900-1930s/Burns-Lucy.htm   Go Links

Lucy Burns

Done

This **Women's Suffrage** site has a wealth of historical photos, including many of the movement's parades, its picketers, and leaders like Lucy Burns.

the fact that he is obstructing the progress of justice and democracy at home while Americans fight for it abroad!"[28] She demanded that the jailbirds be treated as political prisoners because they were jailed for their beliefs, not for committing any crime.

From then on, newspapers kept silent. There was a press blackout of new suffragist activities; it was believed that President Wilson ordered newspapers to ignore the women and their protests.

Paul was placed in solitary confinement for two weeks. She described the prison conditions: "Every window was closed tight. The air in which we were obliged to sleep was foul. . . . There is absolutely no privacy. . . . You are suddenly peered at by curious strangers. . . . Our meals consisted of a little almost raw salt pork, some sort of liquid. . . ."[29] After two weeks, she was too weak to move from her bed. She was taken on a stretcher to the hospital.

Paul went on a hunger strike. She was taken to a psychiatric ward and prison officials

TORTURING WOMEN IN PRISON

VOTE AGAINST THE GOVERNMENT

◁ Jailed suffragists went on hunger strikes to protest their situation. Shown here, women prisoners in Britain were force fed, a painful procedure.

tried to bully her to eat. They threatened to move her to an insane asylum. They examined her and tried to discredit her sanity. She said: "Dr. White took out a small light and held it up to my eyes. Suddenly it dawned upon me that he was examining me personally."[30] Prison officials moved her to the psychiatric ward where they force fed her three times a day for three weeks. They tied her to a chair, forced a tube down her throat, and poured liquid into her until she vomited. Other suffrage prisoners joined the hunger strike when they learned how Paul had been treated.

⊖CRUEL AND UNUSUAL

Forced feedings were a cruel form of punishment. They were not meant to nourish the prisoners. Elizabeth McShane, a former school principal, later reported on the horrors of this treatment:

> . . . Dr. Ladd appeared with a tube that looked like a hose, and a pint of milk in which two eggs had been stirred up. . . . [H]e put the tube in my mouth and told me to swallow it fast . . . but he pushed it down so fast that I gagged and choked terribly. Finally the tube was at what felt like the bottom of my stomach. . . . Then he poured the liquid rapidly down the tube. Of course a stomach that has been unaccustomed to food for a week cannot take so much liquid cold. . . . [I]t began, to come up, out of the corners of my mouth and down my neck until my hair was stiff with it . . . and he walked away, leaving me . . . to die if I chose.[31]

⊖NIGHT OF TERROR

In November 1917, women from different states came to Washington and formed the longest picket line of the campaign. On November 17, President Wilson wrote a memo to an aide about newspaper coverage of the suffragists' activities: "My own suggestion would be that nothing that they do should be featured with headlines or put on the front page, but that a bare, colorless chronicle of what they do should be all that was printed. . . . [I]t need not be made interesting reading."[32]

On November 14, another thirty-three women were arrested and sentenced to as few as six days and as many as six months in jail. That night, the police went into the cells and beat the defenseless women. Lucy Burns was beaten, but received no treatment for her injuries. She was force fed and wrote about it on little pieces of paper smuggled out of the jail: "I was held down by five people at legs, arms, and head. I refused to open mouth. Gannon [the warden] pushed tube up left nostril. . . . It hurts nose and throat very much and makes nose bleed freely."[33]

The authorities tried to hide the brutal treatment of the women, but horror stories leaked out. The public was enraged. A judge determined that it was illegal for the women to be in the district jail. On November 27, President Wilson pardoned the women and they were released.

▲ *Month after month, in rain and cold and every day except Sunday, suffragists picketed in front of the White House. Occasionally, they lit small fires, like the one shown here, in which they burned copies of speeches made by President Wilson that praised democracy in Europe—something American women did not enjoy.*

News of the "Night of Terror," as it came to be known, caused women to flock to Washington to continue picketing. They became more radical and had a new energy. The issue stayed alive during the war. Even more important, the suffrage movement suddenly gained public sympathy.

➔ AND THE WALLS CAME TUMBLING DOWN

On January 9, 1918, President Wilson, under pressure and embarrassed, changed his mind and threw his support behind the amendment. Though an important corner had been turned, the radicals did not stop. They continued to call on Wilson to secure the two votes in Congress that were needed to pass the amendment.

On New Year's Day 1919, there was a new protest while President Wilson was in France negotiating the end of World War I. In his absence, the National Woman's Party placed an urn on the sidewalk in front of the White House and lit a "watchfire of freedom." Into the flames they tossed copies of the President's speeches on democracy that he made while in Europe. One of the protesters said, "The

▽ On August 18, 1920, the Nineteenth Amendment giving women the right to vote was ratified by the required thirty-six (of forty-eight) states. Finally, fifty years after African-American men had been granted the right, American women earned the right to participate in the democratic process.

No. 27,880.   Entered as second-class matter post office Washington, D. C.

SUFFRAGE PROCLAIMED BY COLBY, WHO SIGNS AT HOME EARLY IN DAY

50 = Year Struggle Ends in Victory for Women

NO CEREMONY IN FINAL ACTION

Secretary Felicitates Leaders; Hails New Era.

Ratification of the nineteenth amendment to the Constitution of the United States, granting suffrage to women, was proclaimed officially to-day by Secretary Colby of the State Department.

The proclamation was signed by Secretary Colby at 8 o'clock this morning at his home when the certi-

PROCLAMATION ENFRANCHISES WOMEN OF U. S.

Bainbridge Colby. Secretary of State of the United States of America.

To all to whom these presents shall come, greeting:

Know ye, that the Congress of the United States at the first session, Sixty-sixth Congress, begun at Washington on the nineteenth day of May, in the year one thousand nine hundred and nineteen, passed a resolution as follows, to wit:

Joint resolution, proposing an amendment to the Constitution extending the right of suffrage to women.

Resolved by the Senate and House of Representatives of the United States of America in Congress assembled (two-thirds of each House concurring therein), that the following article is proposed as an amendment to the Constitution, which shall be valid to all intents and purposes as part of the Constitution when ratified by the legislatures of three-fourths of the several states.

White House was empty, but we knew our message would be heard in France."[34] Dozens of women were arrested that month for "building a bonfire on a public highway between sunrise and sunset."

Demonstrations continued. The women showed contempt for President Wilson's weak support. At a massive demonstration on February 9, they burned a portrait of the president. Women who had served time in jail went on a speaking tour, travelling the country in a railroad car called the "Prison Special." Twenty-six former inmates went coast-to-coast telling their stories.

The last public demonstration was on March 4, 1919, in New York City. Twenty-five women carrying banners picketed as President Wilson gave a speech at the Metropolitan Opera House. The crowd and two hundred policemen brutally attacked the protesters, knocking them to the ground and trampling them. Doris Stevens later wrote: "They spoke not a word but beat us back with their clubs with such cruelty as none of us had ever witnessed before."[35] Suffragists were arrested again and released.

➲The Last Vote

At long last, on June 4, 1919, both houses of Congress passed the Nineteenth Amendment and it was sent to the states to be ratified, or formally adopted. Thirty-six states were needed to ratify the amendment. By the summer, thirty-five of thirty-six states had done so. Many southern states firmly opposed the amendment and it seemed doomed. The campaign lasted throughout 1919.

Attention turned to Tennessee, where suffragists and antisuffragists went to influence the legislature. Tennessee was the last state to vote for the amendment and no one was sure how its representatives would vote. The crucial vote was cast by twenty-four-year-old Harry Burn, the youngest member of the legislature. Burn surprised observers by calling out "Aye" for ratification.

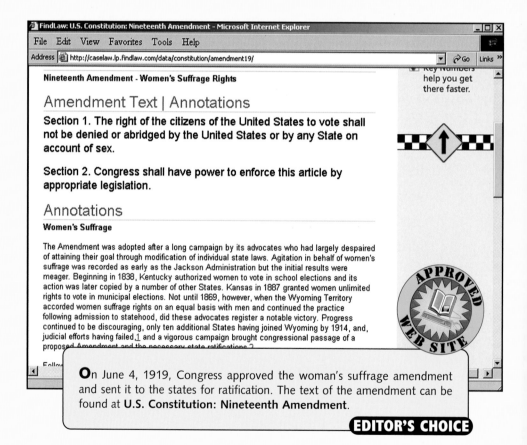

FindLaw: U.S. Constitution: Nineteenth Amendment – Microsoft Internet Explorer

File   Edit   View   Favorites   Tools   Help

Address http://caselaw.lp.findlaw.com/data/constitution/amendment19/   Go   Links »

Nineteenth Amendment - Women's Suffrage Rights

Amendment Text | Annotations

Section 1. The right of the citizens of the United States to vote shall not be denied or abridged by the United States or by any State on account of sex.

Section 2. Congress shall have power to enforce this article by appropriate legislation.

Annotations

Women's Suffrage

The Amendment was adopted after a long campaign by its advocates who had largely despaired of attaining their goal through modification of individual state laws. Agitation in behalf of women's suffrage was recorded as early as the Jackson Administration but the initial results were meager. Beginning in 1838, Kentucky authorized women to vote in school elections and its action was later copied by a number of other States. Kansas in 1887 granted women unlimited rights to vote in municipal elections. Not until 1869, however, when the Wyoming Territory accorded women suffrage rights on an equal basis with men and continued the practice following admission to statehood, did these advocates register a notable victory. Progress continued to be discouraging, only ten additional States having joined Wyoming by 1914, and, judicial efforts having failed,1 and a vigorous campaign brought congressional passage of a proposed Amendment and the necessary state ratifications 2

On June 4, 1919, Congress approved the woman's suffrage amendment and sent it to the states for ratification. The text of the amendment can be found at **U.S. Constitution: Nineteenth Amendment**.

EDITOR'S CHOICE

What none of those in the audience knew was that Burn had a letter in his pocket from Feb Burn, his mother. She urged her son to vote for the amendment. "Dear Son," she wrote, "Hurrah! And vote for suffrage and don't keep them in doubt. . . . Don't forget to be a good boy and help Mrs. Catt put 'Rat' in Ratification."[36]

On August 18, the Nineteenth Amendment giving women the right to vote was ratified. It became law on August 26, 1920—fifty years after African-American men had won the right.

When the first election that allowed women to vote took place on November 2, only one suffragist who had attended the Seneca Falls meeting in 1848 was still alive. Said Charlotte Woodward, "I'm going to vote if they have to carry me there on a stretcher!"[37]

The Nineteenth Amendment more than doubled the number of people who could choose their elected representatives. On November 2, 1920, for the first time in American history, eight million women went to the polls to vote for president, helping elect Warren G. Harding.

3 WHAT DOES THE NINETEENTH AMENDMENT MEAN?

*M*y natural rights, my civil rights, my political rights, my judicial rights, are all alike ignored. Robbed of the fundamental privilege of citizenship, I am degraded from the status of a citizen to that of a subject; and not only myself individually, but all of my sex are, by your Honor's verdict, doomed to political subjection under this, so-called, form of government.

—Susan B. Anthony, found guilty of voting before it was legal for women to do so.[1]

The right to vote is one of the most important aspects of democracy. Voting is the democratic ideal—a democracy cannot exist without the participation of its citizens.

➲ THIRTY-SEVEN POWERFUL WORDS

The Nineteenth Amendment is only thirty-seven words long, but it changed the face of this country. Passed by Congress on June 4, 1919, the actual text of the amendment is simple:

Section 1. The right of citizens of the United States to vote shall not be denied or abridged by the United States or by any State on account of sex.

Section 2. Congress shall have power to enforce this article by appropriate legislation.

▼ *Each time another state ratified the Nineteenth Amendment, Alice Paul (below, center) and members of the National Woman's Party sewed another star on a flag to mark another step toward universal suffrage.*

The amendment guarantees that all citizens of the United States—male *and* female—have the right to vote in state and national elections.

→THE SPREAD OF SUFFRAGE

Before 1920 only a few colonies, territories, and states had constitutions that allowed women to vote. Until the Nineteenth Amendment was ratified, a woman's right to vote depended on the laws of the territory or state in which she lived. A few states that did allow women to vote restricted their participation to certain elections, like school board elections.

Before it became a state, New Jersey's 1776 constitution gave the right to vote to "all free inhabitants," including women. But after claims of voter fraud, the law was rewritten in 1807. The new law aimed to prevent "undesirables" from voting, a category that included women.[2] But until 1838, no state other than New Jersey permitted women to vote in any elections. In that year, Kentucky became the first state to allow widows with children to vote, though only in school elections. Several other states soon followed suit.

In 1869, the Wyoming Territory gave women the right to vote in all elections and continued the practice after becoming a state in 1890. While suffrage slowly spread through the western states, southern and eastern states were slow to follow.

The first four equal suffrage states were Wyoming (1890), Colorado (1893), Utah and Idaho (1896). The movement spread along the west coast and women were granted the vote in Washington (1910), California (1911), and Oregon (1912). Kansas and Arizona followed in 1912. In 1913, Illinois became the first state east of the Mississippi to allow women to vote in a presidential election. In that same year, the Territory of Alaska granted suffrage. The following year Montana and Nevada extended the right.[3] By 1920, there were forty-eight states whose forty-eight different constitutions granted some level of voting rights to women. The Nineteenth Amendment changed all that.

WOMEN NOT INCLUDED

Had the Fourteenth and Fifteenth Amendments been written a bit differently, women would not have had to fight as long and as hard as they did for suffrage.

Indeed, the Fourteenth Amendment states that "All persons born or naturalized in the United States and subject to the jurisdiction thereof are citizens of the United States and of the state wherein they reside." Suffragists claimed they were citizens and therefore could vote. But case

after case, the courts ruled that the Fourteenth
Amendment was designed to give full citizenship
to former slaves, not women. The courts also left
the decision to individual states.

SUFFRAGE AND THE SIXTEENTH AMENDMENT

Suffragists also argued that the Fifteenth Amendment gave them the vote. That amendment,
ratified in 1870, states "The right of citizens of the
United States to vote shall not be denied or
abridged by the United States or by any state on
account of race, color, or previous condition of
servitude." The amendment said that all citizens
had the right to vote. And, of course, women were
citizens. The courts determined that the Fifteenth
Amendment, designed to protect the voting rights
of freed slaves, did not apply to women.

George Washington Julian, of Indiana, first
introduced a national suffrage amendment, the
Sixteenth Amendment, to both houses of Congress
in 1869. The resolution read:

> The right of suffrage in the United States shall be
> based on citizenship, and shall be regulated by
> Congress, and all citizens of the United States,
> whether native or naturalized, shall enjoy this
> right equally, without any distinction or discrimi-
> nation whatever founded on sex.[4]

There were no other changes to the wording of
the amendment until 1880 when suffragists asked

the Senate Judiciary Committee to consider this amendment:

> The right of suffrage in the United States shall be based on citizenship and the right of citizens of the United States to vote shall not be denied or abridged by the United States, or by any State, on account of sex, or for any reason not equally applicable to all citizens of the United States.[5]

The Senate Committee on Woman Suffrage approved this wording. However, the House offered its own version:

> The right of citizens of the United States to vote shall not be denied or abridged by the United States or by any State on account of sex.

The Senate began to consider this version of the amendment in February

In 1890, Carrie Chapman Catt (right) was handpicked by Susan B. Anthony to run one of the first national organizations devoted to women's suffrage. Catt went on to form the League of Women Voters, dedicated to educating women about their new responsibilities as voters.

1885 and it was this version that eventually became the Nineteenth Amendment.[6] But before Congress acted, other constitutional amendments were passed; what could have been the Sixteenth Amendment giving women the right to vote became the Nineteenth Amendment.

→TALLYING THE VOTES IN CONGRESS

Arriving at the number of votes necessary to pass the amendment did not come easy. Both houses of Congress strongly resisted.

The Senate first voted on women's suffrage on January 25, 1887. The resolution was defeated, 34 to 16. The Senate voted for a second time on March 19, 1914, and again, the measure was defeated, 35 to 34. The House of Representatives voted on the amendment for the first time on January 12, 1915, and defeated it, 204 to 174.

On January 9, 1918, President Wilson announced his support of the amendment. The next day, the House of Representatives voted for the second time; this time, the measure passed, 274 to 136. The Senate refused to debate the measure until October.

On October 1, 1918, Wilson addressed the Senate and supported the amendment. That same day and for the third time, the Senate defeated it, 62 to 34. As a result, the National Woman's Party urged citizens to vote against all anti-suffragist senators who were running for election that year. After the 1918 election, most members of Congress supported women's suffrage.

On February 10, 1919, the Senate defeated the amendment for a fourth time, 63 to 33. A few months later, the House voted in favor of the amendment, 304 to 89. Finally and at long last on June 4, 1919, the Senate passed the amendment, 66 to 30.[7]

It was now in the hands of each state to ratify the amendment—and on August 18, 1920, the last of the necessary thirty-six (of forty-eight) states did (Alaska and Hawaii were not yet part of the United States). Some states were slow to ratify—for

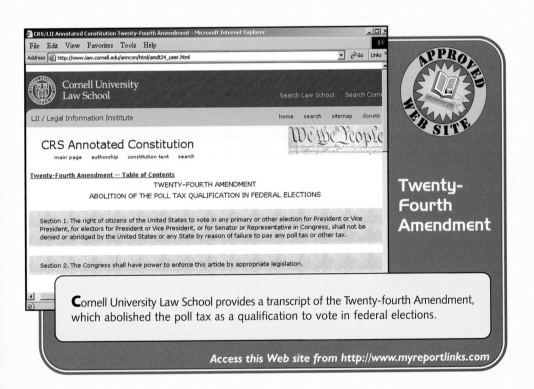

Cornell University Law School provides a transcript of the Twenty-fourth Amendment, which abolished the poll tax as a qualification to vote in federal elections.

Access this Web site from http://www.myreportlinks.com

example, Maryland did not do so until 1941. Nevertheless, on August 26, 1920, Secretary of State Bainbridge Colby certified the ratification and the amendment became law. That date is still celebrated as "Women's Equality Day."

Carrie Chapman Catt, a prominent leader of the women's suffrage movement, described the obstacles in getting the Nineteenth Amendment passed:

> To get the word male . . . out of the constitution cost the women of the country fifty-two years of pauseless [continuous] campaign . . . . During that time they were forced to conduct fifty-six campaigns of referenda to male voters; 480 campaigns to urge Legislatures to submit suffrage amendments to voters; 47 campaigns to induce State constitutional conventions to write woman suffrage into State constitutions; 277 campaigns to persuade State party conventions to include woman suffrage planks; 30 campaigns to urge presidential party conventions to adopt woman suffrage planks in party platforms, and 19 campaigns with 19 successive Congresses.[8]

⊜THEN AND NOW

Despite everything, the ratification of the Nineteenth Amendment did not mean all women could suddenly vote. In theory, all women should have had access to the polls, but they did not. As hard as it was to change the law, it was even harder to change the ideas and customs of people—especially when it came to African-American women. They faced obstacles that white women did not. Few, if any, black women registered to vote. And things like literacy tests and poll taxes prevented them from even registering.

These obstacles were finally eliminated in the 1960s—the Twenty-fourth Amendment, which was passed in 1964 and outlawed poll taxes, said that neither the United States nor individual states can force a citizen to pay a tax in order to vote. And the Voting Rights Act of 1965 eliminated literacy as a voting requirement. Finally, the Twenty-sixth Amendment, passed in 1971, lowered the voting age from twenty-one to eighteen. This was a reaction to the Vietnam War, when some people argued that if an eighteen-year-old could die in war, then an eighteen-year-old was certainly old enough to vote.

➲ Voting Rights versus Equal Rights

Traditionally, women's movements have led to political and social rights for women. When the Nineteenth Amendment passed, most women suffragists were elated. They had won, their work was finished. But that is a narrow interpretation of what the amendment meant.

Many women felt that winning the right to vote was not the goal, but rather a first step. They saw the suffrage movement as a small-but-important part of a broader struggle to achieve equal rights. They wanted to expand the interpretation of the Nineteenth Amendment. Alice Paul was once again at the forefront. She immediately began working for another amendment to the Constitution—in 1923, she wrote an Equal Rights Amendment to guarantee equal treatment for women and men.

TESTING THE LIMITS 4

*I*n their struggle to win the right to vote, American suffragists waged battles at all levels of society. They even challenged in the courts, arguing cases at both the state and federal level and before the U.S. Supreme Court. In the early cases, women lost, which seemed to reinforce the idea that women were inferior to men.

→ *BRADWELL* V. *ILLINOIS* (1872)

Although not expressly about a woman's right to vote, this case is the first heard by the U.S. Supreme Court that dealt with sex discrimination against women.

According to the U.S. Census, in 1870 there were about five female lawyers in the country.[1] One of them, Myra Bradwell, had studied law and passed the test to be admitted to the Chicago Bar. But the Illinois Supreme Court said she could not practice law. Why? Because she was married.

Mrs. Bradwell appealed the decision to the Supreme Court. Like all court cases, this one was named for those who are on opposite sides in a case: *Bradwell* v. *Illinois,* in which Bradwell was the plaintiff, or the person

After all is said and done, it is up to the nine justices of the U.S. Supreme Court to interpret how Constitutional amendments are applied to everyday life. The court constantly hears cases that challenge the legal underpinnings of certain amendments.

suing in court. The state of Illinois was the defendant, the person or party being sued. Mrs. Bradwell argued that her right to practice law was protected by the Fourteenth Amendment. The Supreme Court disagreed. One of the justices, Joseph P. Bradley, said in his opinion:

> The natural and proper timidity and delicacy which belongs to the female sex evidently unfits it for many occupations of civil life. . . . [A] married woman is incapable, without her husband's consent, of making contracts . . . a married woman [is] incompetent fully to perform the duties and trusts that belong to the office of an attorney and counsellor. . . . The paramount destiny and mission of woman are to fulfill the noble and benign offices of wife and mother. This is the law of the Creator.[2]

The Court said that not only did the state laws of Illinois prevent Mrs. Bradwell from being a licensed attorney, but that the laws of a Supreme Power also prevented her. This was a crushing defeat for women.

➔ *MINOR V. HAPPERSETT* (1874)

In October 1872, Virginia Minor, of Missouri, tried to register to vote in the election for president. She believed it was her right as a citizen. But she lived in Missouri, a state that did not allow women to vote (married women in Missouri could not even sue without the consent of their husbands).

Reese Happersett, the state registrar of voters, prevented Mrs. Minor from voting because she was a woman. Francis Minor, Virginia's husband, filed suit against Mr. Happersett in the state court of Missouri on behalf of his wife.

Mr. and Mrs. Minor were members of the National American Woman Suffrage Association

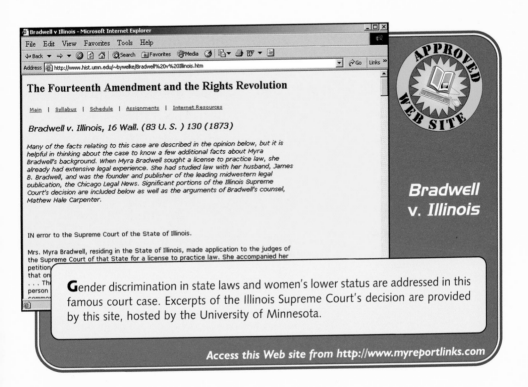

Gender discrimination in state laws and women's lower status are addressed in this famous court case. Excerpts of the Illinois Supreme Court's decision are provided by this site, hosted by the University of Minnesota.

Access this Web site from http://www.myreportlinks.com

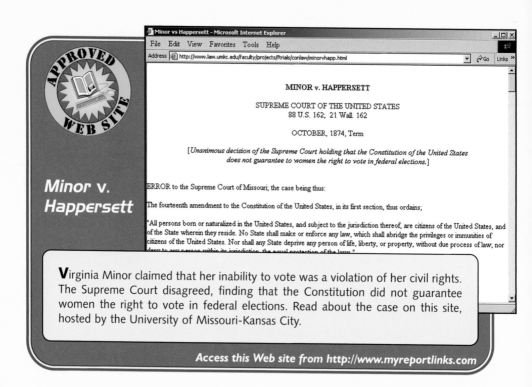

MINOR v. HAPPERSETT

SUPREME COURT OF THE UNITED STATES
88 U.S. 162; 21 Wall. 162

OCTOBER, 1874, Term

[*Unanimous decision of the Supreme Court holding that the Constitution of the United States does not guarantee to women the right to vote in federal elections.*]

ERROR to the Supreme Court of Missouri; the case being thus:

The fourteenth amendment to the Constitution of the United States, in its first section, thus ordains;

"All persons born or naturalized in the United States, and subject to the jurisdiction thereof, are citizens of the United States, and of the State wherein they reside. No State shall make or enforce any law, which shall abridge the privileges or immunities of citizens of the United States. Nor shall any State deprive any person of life, liberty, or property, without due process of law; nor

Virginia Minor claimed that her inability to vote was a violation of her civil rights. The Supreme Court disagreed, finding that the Constitution did not guarantee women the right to vote in federal elections. Read about the case on this site, hosted by the University of Missouri-Kansas City.

Access this Web site from http://www.myreportlinks.com

(NAWAS), which encouraged women to vote under the Fourteenth Amendment. Mr. Minor argued that his wife had the right to vote because the amendment gave that right to U.S. citizens. He claimed that the registrar deprived his wife of her legal right. The Missouri court dismissed the case.

In 1874, Mr. and Mrs. Minor petitioned the U.S. Supreme Court. The Court listened to the arguments in *Minor* v. *Happersett* and made a unanimous decision in favor of the state of Missouri. Chief Justice Morris Waite said that women were both citizens and persons in the eyes of the Constitution, but that as women they enjoyed a special status that did not include the right to vote.

States could deny women the right to vote because neither the Constitution nor the Fourteenth Amendment required states to allow women the vote.

"Being unanimously of the opinion that the Constitution of the United States does not confer the right of suffrage upon any one," wrote the Court, "and that the constitutions and laws of the several States which commit that important trust to men alone are not necessarily void, we Affirm the [state] judgment."[3]

This case is important for two reasons. The Supreme Court ruled that the Fourteenth Amendment did not grant women the right to vote and, further, that suffrage was not a right, but a privilege

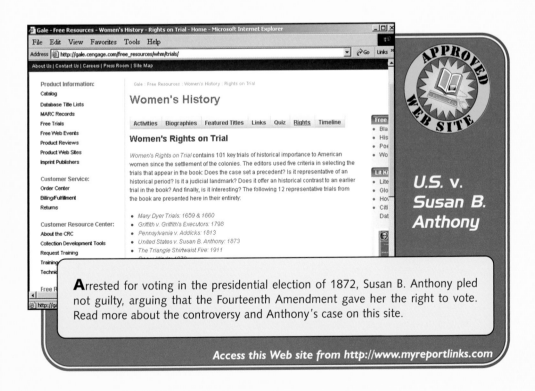

U.S. v. Susan B. Anthony

Arrested for voting in the presidential election of 1872, Susan B. Anthony pled not guilty, arguing that the Fourteenth Amendment gave her the right to vote. Read more about the controversy and Anthony's case on this site.

Access this Web site from http://www.myreportlinks.com

given by each state legislature. In other words, each state had the right to make its own decisions on voting. Eventually the Nineteenth Amendment would reverse the outcome of this case.

→ UNITED STATES V. SUSAN B. ANTHONY (1873)

In 1871 and 1872, American women were urged to challenge the interpretation of the Fourteenth and Fifteenth Amendments by going to the polls and voting. Suffragists hoped to use the federal courts to test the limits of each amendment.

On November 1, 1872, about the same time that Virginia Minor was trying to vote in Missouri, Susan B. Anthony led a group of women to register to vote in her hometown of Rochester. Election inspectors refused, but Anthony bullied them into letting her register. Early on November 5, Anthony and fourteen other women went to the polling place and cast their ballots for president of the United States.[4]

Sylvester Lewis, a Rochester resident, filed a complaint charging Anthony with casting an illegal vote. The United States commissioner, William C. Storrs, issued a warrant for Anthony's arrest. He charged her with voting in a federal election "without having a lawful right to vote" and violating the Enforcement Act of Congress, which carried a penalty of five hundred dollars and three years in jail.

On November 18, the fifty-two-year-old Anthony was arrested. At her hearing, she refused to pay the five-hundred-dollar bail and Commissioner Storrs ordered her held until a grand jury could meet and consider the case. Her lawyer applied for a writ of habeas corpus saying that Anthony had not violated any laws. Habeas corpus is a legal term that means that an accused person must be presented physically before the court with a statement that shows sufficient cause for arrest. It protects people from being held in prison unlawfully.

The U.S. district judge denied the writ of habeas corpus and increased bail to one thousand dollars. Henry Selden, Anthony's lawyer, put up the bail and she was released. Anthony was not pleased; in fact she was furious that she lost her chance to take her case to the U.S. Supreme Court.

Her trial on June 17, 1873, packed the courtroom. Judge Ward Hunt, known to be an opponent of women's suffrage,

To honor Susan B. Anthony on what would have been her 109th birthday in 1929, members of the National Council of the Woman's Party place a wreath at a statue that depicts (from right) Lucretia Mott, Anthony, and Elizabeth Cady Stanton.

presided. Anthony's main argument was that she reasonably believed that she was eligible to vote and could not be guilty of the crime of "knowingly" casting an illegal ballot.

GUILTY OF BEING A WOMAN

Anthony's attorney called her as a witness to testify, but the prosecution objected: "She is not a competent as a witness on her own behalf."[5] That meant she was not allowed to testify at her own trial because she was a woman.

Selden opened his three-hour long argument:

> If the same act had been done by her brother under the same circumstances, the act would have been not only innocent, but honorable and laudable; but having been done by a woman it is said to be a crime. The crime therefore consists not in the act done, but in the simple fact that the person doing it was a woman and not a man, I believe this is the first instance in which a woman has been arraigned in a criminal court, merely on account of her sex. . . .[6]

The right to a trial by jury for a criminal act is guaranteed under the law. But immediately after both sides gave their closing arguments, Judge Ward Hunt read his opinion: "The Fourteenth Amendment gives no right to a woman to vote, and the voting by Miss Anthony was in violation of the law. . . . Upon this evidence I suppose there is no question for the jury and that the jury should be directed to find a verdict of guilty."[7] He had taken the decision out of the jury's hands. When the clerk of the court asked the jury its verdict, the members remained silent. Judge Hunt dismissed the jury and found Anthony guilty.

In Her Own Defense

The judge asked Anthony if she had anything to say before he sentenced her. She seized this golden opportunity to speak about her treatment under the legal system, stunning the courtroom. Anthony would not be silenced whenever the judge tried to interrupt her. "But Your Honor will not deny me this one and only poor privilege of protest against this high-handed outrage upon my citizen's rights," she declared. ". . . [T]his is the first time that either myself or any person of my disfranchised class has been allowed a word of defense before judge or jury."[8]

Judge Hunt fined her one hundred dollars. She refused to pay. The judge decided he would not send her to jail until her fine was paid. She never paid it. Her eight-month legal battle, a widely-publicized trial that gained national attention and public support, kept the issue of women's suffrage in the news.

Virginia Minor's defeat and Anthony's arrest marked a turning point in the movement—suffragists stopped challenging the Fourteenth and Fifteenth Amendments in court. Instead they went to work to create a new national amendment that would give them the right to vote.

→ HARLAND V. WASHINGTON (1887)

In 1883, the Washington Territory extended the vote to women who lived in the territory—including and for the first time in American history, African-American women. It was one of the most liberal voting laws in the nation.

Jefferson Harland had been convicted of illegal gambling by a jury that included five women. He appealed the verdict, claiming it was illegal for women to serve as jurors and to vote. The case went up to the Territorial Supreme Court of Washington. The court agreed and reversed his conviction. The court even struck down the law that allowed women to vote, saying it was unconstitutional. The decision might have been unfair, but it was the law.[9]

→ LESER V. GARNETT (1922)

After the Nineteenth Amendment was ratified by Congress in 1920, the anti-suffragists, hoping the courts would find the amendment illegal, brought several cases to trial.

In 1922, Oscar Leser, a former judge and an antisuffragist, brought suit along with other people in the Maryland Court of Common Pleas (the case was called *Leser* v. *Garnett* because Leser was the first person listed on the lawsuit). They wanted women removed from the list of eligible voters. They claimed the Nineteenth Amendment was unconstitutional on three grounds. First, it was not authorized by Article V of the U.S. Constitution, which describes two ways in which the Constitution may be amended. Second, the amendment was never legally ratified by the legislatures of three-fourths of the states. And finally, the amendment was rejected by the Maryland legislature.

The court denied the suit and held that the Nineteenth Amendment was valid. Leser appealed the case and the Maryland Court of Appeals agreed with the lower court. Leser took the case to the Supreme Court, which upheld the two previous opinions. The Supreme Court ruled that

In an effort to convince ▶ women to help settle the western United States in the nineteenth century, some territories granted women the right to vote. This weekly newspaper from 1888 shows women in the Wyoming Territory casting ballots.

WOMAN SUFFRAGE IN WYOMING TERRITORY—SCENE AT THE POLLS IN CHEYENNE.

the Nineteenth Amendment was valid, a blow to the anti-suffragists.[10]

BREEDLOVE V. SUTTLES (1937)

The U.S. Supreme Court has heard only one case concerning the effect of the Nineteenth Amendment.[11] The Court ruled that the Nineteenth Amendment applies to women and men alike. *Breedlove* v. *Suttles* is about the poll tax.

In 1934, the state of Georgia required eligible voters between the age of twenty-one and sixty to pay a one-dollar poll tax every year. The tax was collected when people registered to vote; if their tax was not paid, they could not vote. The tax did not apply to blind people or any females who did not register to vote.

Nolan Breedlove, a twenty-eight-year-old white male, did not pay. He tried to register to vote at the primary and general elections, but Mr. Suttles, the tax collector, refused. Breedlove was denied the right to vote. Breedlove sued, claiming the tax was illegal because it conflicted with the equal protection clause and the privilege and immunity clause of the Fourteenth Amendment and was against the Nineteenth Amendment.

The county court and state supreme court in Georgia rejected his claim. Breedlove appealed to the U.S. Supreme Court, which agreed with the lower courts: The Georgia poll tax was legal. It said that because it applies to all races, the tax does not violate the Fourteenth or Fifteenth Amendments. It said the law did not discriminate against men by giving a partial exemption to women. The Court also said each state has the right to make its own decisions on who can vote.[12]

Although the taxes of one dollar per year may seem small, it was a lot of money for many poor white and African-American men. The underlying purpose of the tax was not to collect money, but to prevent former slaves from voting. The verdict in this case was a setback for voting rights, especially for African-American men and women.

➔ *HARPER* V. *VIRGINIA STATE BOARD OF ELECTIONS* (1966)

The state of Virginia had a yearly poll tax of $1.50 on all residents over the age of twenty-one. Of that amount, one dollar went to public schools and fifty cents for general-purpose use. Annie E. Harper sued the state board of elections. She claimed the poll tax was unconstitutional. A lower court dismissed the case and Mrs. Harper took her case to the U.S. Supreme Court.

The Court found in favor of Mrs. Harper. The Court said: ". . . the right to vote is too precious, too fundamental to be so burdened or conditioned." In other words, the right to vote is not based on a person's ability to pay a poll tax.[13] This case, which outlawed poll taxes in state and local elections, was decided two years after the Twenty-fourth Amendment, which banned poll taxes in federal elections, was ratified in 1964.

→ *LASSITER V. NORTHAMPTON COUNTY BOARD OF ELECTIONS* (1959)

Before the 1960s, many states and municipalities used literacy tests as a way to prevent African Americans from voting. The state of North Carolina forced residents to take a literacy test to prove

Not For Ourselves Alone, a PBS Web site, provides a history of the nineteenth century women's rights campaign and includes biographies of many of the leading women, and essays on the suffrage movement.

EDITOR'S CHOICE

The Voting Rights Act Of 1965 - Microsoft Internet Explorer

File   Edit   View   Favorites   Tools   Help

Address http://www.usdoj.gov/crt/voting/intro/intro_c.htm   Go   Links »

**United States Department of Justice
Civil Rights Division
Voting Section**

Introduction To Federal Voting Rights Laws

- Introduction To Federal Voting Rights Laws
- Before the Voting Rights Act
- The Voting Rights Act of 1965
- The Effect of the Voting Rights Act

The Effect of the Voting Rights Act

Soon after passage of the Voting Rights Act, federal examiners were conducting voter registration, and black voter registration began a sharp increase. The cumulative effect of the Supreme Court's decisions, Congress' enactment of voting rights leg...

**Federal
Voting
Rights
Laws**

Initially adopted in 1965, the Voting Rights Act is one of the most important pieces of civil rights legislation ever ratified. The U.S. Department of Justice hosts a site that has an overview of the Act, as well as text of Amendments to it passed in 1970, 1975, and 1982.

Access this Web site from http://www.myreportlinks.com

they could read or write in order to vote. Louise Lassiter, an African-American woman, could not register to vote or serve on juries. She claimed the test violated her constitutional rights.

The Supreme Court ruled that literacy tests for voting in North Carolina were legal because they applied equally to all races. The Court said the requirement to "be able to read and write any section of the Constitution of North Carolina in the English language," did not violate the Fifteenth Amendment.[14] The case was decided before Congress passed the Voting Rights Act in 1965, which banned literacy tests in state elections. *Lassiter* v. *Northampton* was overturned by the new law.

5   A Living Document

*T*he United States Constitution is often referred to as a living document—it was not written as a set of definite rules that must be followed forever to the letter. Instead, it was designed to be interpreted, allowed to reflect the changing ideas of American society.

The Nineteenth Amendment granted voting rights to American women, but not full and equal legal rights. In their struggle to gain equal rights with men, American women have challenged discrimination in a wide variety of cases. Some have made it to the Supreme Court. For the first one hundred years after the Bradwell case, the Supreme Court agreed with state courts that put restrictions on women.[1] But by the 1950s, women began winning some of the cases. And around 1970, the Supreme Court began using the Equal Protection Clause of the Fourteenth Amendment to challenge state laws that discriminated against women's citizenship and rights.[2]

Over the decades, the Supreme Court has heard these cases often with conflicting results. The

Constitution of the United States of America - Official - Microsoft Internet Explorer

File   Edit   View   Favorites   Tools   Help

Address http://www.archives.gov/national-archives-experience/charters/constitution.html   Go   Links »

THE NATIONAL ARCHIVES EXPERIENCE

MAIN PAGE   VISIT US   CHARTERS OF FREEDOM   NEWS AND EVENTS   SUPPORT THE ARCHIVES

MAKING OF THE CHARTERS   THE DECLARATION OF INDEPENDENCE   THE CONSTITUTION   THE BILL OF RIGHTS   IMPACT OF THE CHARTERS   HIGH-RESOLUTION IMAGES

◄ previous

the Charters of Freedom
"A NEW WORLD IS AT HAND"

next ▶

MAKING OF THE CHARTERS   IMPACT OF THE CHARTERS

Constitution of the United States

view larger images ▶   read transcript ▶   download high-resolution images ▶   more resources

APPROVED WEB SITE

The Charters of Freedom Web site has the transcript as well as a photo of the U.S. Constitution. Learn how this important document came to be written, read each amendment, and discover interesting details about the Constitution.

EDITOR'S CHOICE

Court has sometimes expanded, or sometimes limited women in their struggle for equal rights. Many issues are still debated today. Laws have discriminated against women in almost every aspect of society, including domestic relations (marriage and the family); educational opportunities; employment; as well as civic and social affairs.

CIVIL DUTIES: JURY SERVICE

For decades after winning the right to vote, most women were still excluded from the legal system.

In most states, women could not serve on juries, which meant that when women were tried for a crime, they did not face a jury of their peers. After the Nineteenth Amendment was passed, and women fought to gain truly equal rights with men, jury duty was one of the first areas they wanted to reform. The following three cases show how the Supreme Court has modified its opinion on whether or not women have the right to serve on juries.

➔ JURY DUTY

In *Glasser* v. *United States* (1942), Mr. Glasser, an assistant U.S. Attorney, was convicted of defrauding the United States in handling liquor cases. He appealed the verdict, claiming the jury had not been drawn from a fair sampling of the community. The pool of possible female jurors came from a list maintained by the League of Women Voters, a civic organization. The Supreme Court dismissed his claim, ruling that the Nineteenth Amendment did not automatically make women eligible to serve on juries.[3]

Almost twenty years later the Court heard *Hoyt* v. *Florida* (1961), in which Ms. Gwendolyn Hoyt was charged in Florida with murdering her husband. She pleaded not guilty because of "temporary insanity." A jury of twelve men found her guilty. In Florida, women had to volunteer

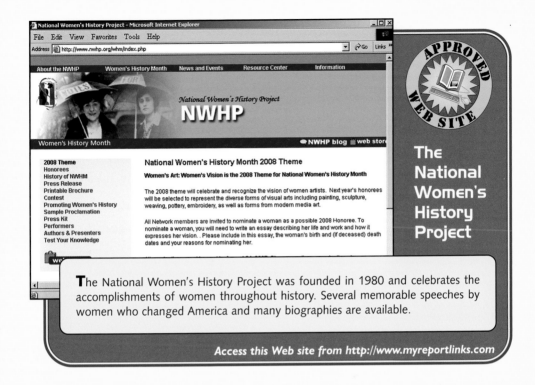

National Women's History Project - Microsoft Internet Explorer

File Edit View Favorites Tools Help

Address http://www.nwhp.org/whm/index.php

About the NWHP   Women's History Month   News and Events   Resource Center   Information

National Women's History Project
NWHP

Women's History Month   NWHP blog   web store

2008 Theme
Honorees
History of NWHM
Press Release
Printable Brochure
Contest
Promoting Women's History
Sample Proclamation
Press Kit
Performers
Authors & Presenters
Test Your Knowledge

National Women's History Month 2008 Theme

Women's Art: Women's Vision is the 2008 Theme for National Women's History Month

The 2008 theme will celebrate and recognize the vision of women artists. Next year's honorees will be selected to represent the diverse forms of visual arts including painting, sculpture, weaving, pottery, embroidery, as well as forms from modern media art.

All Network members are invited to nominate a woman as a possible 2008 Honoree. To nominate a woman, you will need to write an essay describing her life and work and how it expresses her vision. . Please include in this essay, the woman's birth and (if deceased) death dates and your reasons for nominating her.

APPROVED WEB SITE

The National Women's History Project

The National Women's History Project was founded in 1980 and celebrates the accomplishments of women throughout history. Several memorable speeches by women who changed America and many biographies are available.

Access this Web site from http://www.myreportlinks.com

for jury duty; state law did not require them to register.

Ms. Hoyt argued that female jurors would have been more sympathetic to her. The Supreme Court upheld the Florida laws that kept women from jury duty unless they volunteered. In a unanimous decision, the Court noted that even though women were "still regarded as the center and home of family life" they were legally excused from civic duties.[4]

By 1975, the Court had altered its thinking. In *Taylor* v. *Louisiana,* the defendant, Billy J. Taylor was convicted of aggravated kidnapping. An all-male jury was chosen from an all-male pool. In

Louisiana, a state that had similar jury duty laws to Florida, women had to register their desire to serve in writing. The Supreme Court reversed *Hoyt* v. *Florida* and said that the state law that excluded women from jury service was unconstitutional. Therefore, Mr. Taylor had been deprived of his constitutional right to "a fair trial by jury of a representative segment of the community," in part because only a few women from the community volunteered to serve.

The Court went on to note the changing role of women, saying "the day has long passed" when women were viewed in a "special position" and "that society cannot spare *any* women from their present duties." The Court made it a requirement that women serve on juries in state courts.[5]

→ EMPLOYMENT: *WEEKS* V. *SOUTHERN BELL TEL. AND TEL.* (1969)

In the early 1960s, Congress passed two laws that significantly changed the status of women in society. In 1963, it passed the Equal Pay Act (EPA) which basically said that women should be paid the same amount of money that a man is paid for doing the same work. The act has become known as "equal work, equal pay." The following year, Congress passed Title VII of the Civil Rights Act, which banned discrimination based on race, color, religion, national origin, or sex. It was a major victory for women in their fight against sex discrimination.

Though there would be many cases that challenged discrimination against women in the workplace, *Weeks* v. *Southern Bell Tel. and Tel.,* was the first.

Mrs. Lorena W. Weeks applied for a job as a switchman at work. She could not be promoted because a state law said women could not lift objects weighing more than thirty pounds. She sued because Southern Bell promoted a less senior male to a job that required "strenuous" labor— lifting a thirty-four pound fire extinguisher. The lower court ruled against Mrs. Weeks.

She appealed to a circuit court of appeals. The court criticized Southern Bell for its policies against women, saying the company's policy violated the Civil Rights Act of 1964. It ruled that women have the "power to decide if they should take on unromantic tasks," opening the door to jobs that historically had been reserved for men.[6]

➔ FAMILY LAW: *REED* V. *REED* (1971)

The U.S. Supreme Court has also extended women's rights regarding domestic life. The case of *Reed* v. *Reed* shows how family law has changed to give women more legal rights.

Sally Reed was a divorced mother of a teenage son. While her son was at his father's house, he

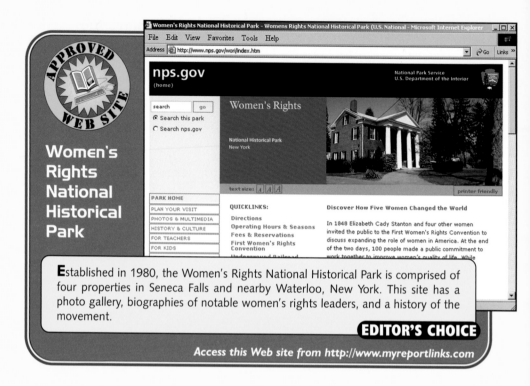

Women's Rights National Historical Park

nps.gov
(home)

National Park Service
U.S. Department of the Interior

Women's Rights

National Historical Park
New York

search   go
⊙ Search this park
○ Search nps.gov

text size: A A A   printer friendly

PARK HOME
PLAN YOUR VISIT
PHOTOS & MULTIMEDIA
HISTORY & CULTURE
FOR TEACHERS
FOR KIDS

QUICKLINKS:

Directions
Operating Hours & Seasons
Fees & Reservations
First Women's Rights
Convention

Discover How Five Women Changed the World

In 1848 Elizabeth Cady Stanton and four other women
invited the public to the First Women's Rights Convention to
discuss expanding the role of women in America. At the end
of the two days, 100 people made a public commitment to
work together to improve women's quality of life. While

Established in 1980, the Women's Rights National Historical Park is comprised of four properties in Seneca Falls and nearby Waterloo, New York. This site has a photo gallery, biographies of notable women's rights leaders, and a history of the movement.

EDITOR'S CHOICE

Access this Web site from http://www.myreportlinks.com

died in an apparent suicide by using his father's gun. He died without a will. Sally Reed wanted to be the administrator of her son's small estate; so did the boy's father. The Idaho court appointed the father, following a state law that said "males must be preferred to females" when choosing between two people who are equally entitled to the estate.

Ms. Reed challenged the state law. The Supreme Court unanimously held that the state law of Idaho violated women's rights under the Equal Protection Clause. This was the first time the Supreme Court struck down a state law that treated men and women differently. Finally, the court defined women as "persons."[7]

➔ CIVIC RIGHTS: *ROSTKER V. GOLDBERG* (1981)

In 1980, President Jimmy Carter reinstated the draft registration—when men turned eighteen, they were required to register for possible military service. At the same time, he wanted to change the policy to include women. Congress voted against his recommendation, because women were not allowed to serve in combat.

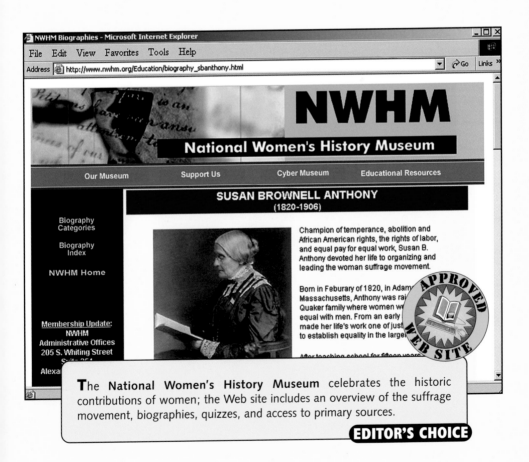

The **National Women's History Museum** celebrates the historic contributions of women; the Web site includes an overview of the suffrage movement, biographies, quizzes, and access to primary sources.

EDITOR'S CHOICE

Robert Goldberg and several others challenged the draft in the case *Rostker* v. *Goldberg* (1981), arguing that the men-only draft was unconstitutional under the Due Process Clause of the Fifth Amendment. Goldberg believed the draft discriminated against men on the basis of gender.

The Supreme Court ruled that it was constitutional to exclude women from registering because they were not allowed in combat. Because the draft was not based on gender, it was not against Due Process laws. To date, women are not permitted to serve in special forces and cannot serve in the infantry.[8]

▼ Gussie Ann Lord (below) became one of the first twenty three women to earn recognition as a full cadet at the Virginia Military Institute after the U.S. Supreme Court ruled in 1996 that the all-male school must admit women.

⊖ Social Rights: *Roberts v. United States Jaycees* (1984)

Women gained more social rights as they fought for membership in groups that once admitted only men. In the case of *Roberts v. United States Jaycees* (1984), the Supreme Court decided that the United States Jaycees, a not-for-profit organization, must allow women to become full members. The decision reaffirmed that "sex discrimination will not be accepted in the public marketplace." This made it possible for women to join other organizations that had been all male.[9]

⊖ Education: *United States v. Virginia* (1996)

The Virginia Military Institute (VMI), founded in 1839 and operated by the state of Virginia, had a policy that said only men could be admitted to the school. In 1996, the U.S. Department of Justice filed suit, claiming the school's admission policy violated the Fourteenth Amendment. In 1972, Congress passed Title IX of the Education Amendments Act, prohibiting sex discrimination in all education programs that receive federal money. The Supreme Court found that excluding women from state-supported schools violated the Fourteenth Amendment. As a result, thirty female cadets entered VMI in 1996.[10]

6 DO WOMEN REALLY HAVE THE SAME RIGHTS AS MEN?

ighty years after passage of the Nineteenth Amendment, women continue to meet new challenges in their struggle to be equal with men.

→ EQUAL RIGHTS AMENDMENT (ERA)

Once women gained the vote, the women's movement changed. Carrie Chapman Catt formed the League of Women Voters (LWV), designed to educate new voters about their responsibilities (the league continues to educate and register voters). In contrast, Alice Paul believed that the Nineteenth Amendment was just a first step, that women were still denied basic rights enjoyed by men. She and her National Woman's Party rejected women's traditional role and aimed to extend women's rights in political and social life.

A new women's movement began with the Equal Rights Amendment (ERA), the brainchild of Paul. She introduced the amendment in 1923 at the seventy-fifth

The Web site of the League of Women Voters has a large online library containing photographs, reports, and full-text copies of its bi-monthly publication the "National Voter."

Access this Web site from http://www.myreportlinks.com

anniversary of the Seneca Falls convention. It is also known as the Lucretia Mott Amendment, after one of the Seneca Falls pioneers.

The Equal Rights Amendment had been introduced into every session of Congress from 1923 to 1970. The text, as presented in 1972 to the Ninety-second Congress is as follows:

Section 1. Equality of rights under the law shall not be denied or abridged by the United States or by any State on account of sex.

Section 2. The Congress shall have the power to enforce, by appropriate legislation, the provisions of this article.

The Equal Rights Amendment

The Equal Rights Amendment

Equality of rights under the law shall not be denied or

Overview
History
FAQ
Why
Strategy
Legislation
Political Status
Supporters

The ERA in Congress

ERA bills reintroduced in Congress on March 27, 2007:

★ SJRes 10
★ HJRes 40

★★★★★

RECENT RESEARCH

Although first introduced in 1923, the Equal Rights Amendment was not passed by Congress until 1972. Visit this site for information and a more recent history of the Amendment, which was never ratified.

Access this Web site from http://www.myreportlinks.com

Section 3. This amendment shall take effect two years after the date of ratification.

Both houses of Congress passed the ERA on March 22, 1972, and sent it to the state legislatures for ratification. Congress attached a seven-year time limit for ratification, which it later extended to June 30, 1982. Three more states were needed to ratify it, but the time limit ran out and the amendment expired. Opponents claimed it would have taken away important legal protections for women. After its defeat, the women's rights movement once again looked to the courts and the ballot box to gain and to keep what they felt were their constitutional rights.

A SECOND WIND

Inspired by the Civil Rights movement, the women's movement was energized in the 1960s, turning its attention to equality in work, family, and politics. In 1961, President John F. Kennedy set up the Presidential Commission on the Status of Women and appointed former first lady Eleanor Roosevelt to the board.

The women's movement was also reawakened in part by a book written by Betty Friedan called *The Feminine Mystique.* Friedan, who was a writer, wife, and mother, wrote that women wanted to do something more with their lives than become wives and mothers. Women could help themselves,

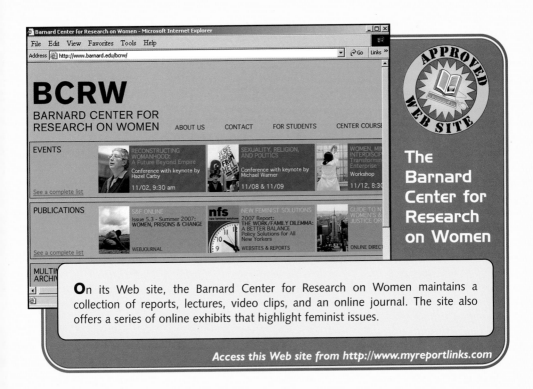

On its Web site, the Barnard Center for Research on Women maintains a collection of reports, lectures, video clips, and an online journal. The site also offers a series of online exhibits that highlight feminist issues.

Access this Web site from http://www.myreportlinks.com

▲ *The women's movement was reinvigorated in the 1960s, in part because of Betty Friedan's book,* The Feminine Mystique. *Originally published in 1963, the book examined women's role in society. In the late 1960s, Friedan helped found a few leading feminist organizations, including the National Organization for Women.*

she believed, by looking beyond their traditional roles. The book struck a nerve with women.

In 1966, Friedan and other feminists founded the National Organization of Women (NOW) to secure and defend women's legal rights. The organization is still the backbone of the feminist movement. When NOW came on the scene, yet another group emerged. These women were younger and more defiant than the women of NOW. They wanted more than equality; they wanted freedom from all institutions that oppressed women. These young feminists took a page from Alice Paul's book and used radical tactics to make headlines, including speak-outs and demonstrations. In 1968, they protested the Miss America pageant in Atlantic City, New Jersey, arguing that the contest valued a woman's beauty more than it did her intelligence.

As a result of the feminist movement, women began to achieve breakthroughs in just about every area of society. Women have made slow-but-steady advances and become part of the group known as America's decision makers. Today, more and more women hold positions of influence as CEOs of Fortune 500 companies, presidents of major universities, and advisors to presidents.

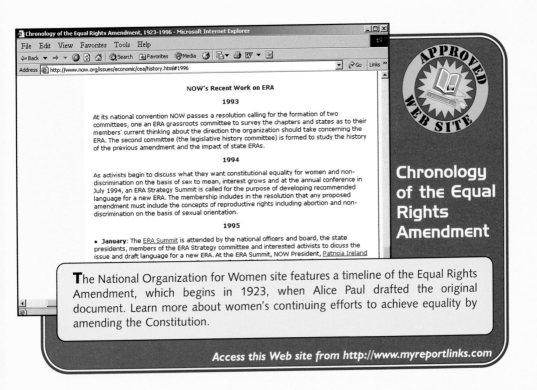

Chronology of the Equal Rights Amendment, 1923-1996 - Microsoft Internet Explorer

File   Edit   View   Favorites   Tools   Help

Back   Search   Favorites   Media

Address   http://www.now.org/issues/economic/cea/history.html#1996

NOW's Recent Work on ERA

1993

At its national convention NOW passes a resolution calling for the formation of two committees, one an ERA grassroots committee to survey the chapters and states as to their members' current thinking about the direction the organization should take concerning the ERA. The second committee (the legislative history committee) is formed to study the history of the previous amendment and the impact of state ERAs.

1994

As activists begin to discuss what they want constitutional equality for women and non-discrimination on the basis of sex to mean, interest grows and at the annual conference in July 1994, an ERA Strategy Summit is called for the purpose of developing recommended language for a new ERA. The membership includes in the resolution that any proposed amendment must include the concepts of reproductive rights including abortion and non-discrimination on the basis of sexual orientation.

1995

• **January:** The ERA Summit is attended by the national officers and board, the state presidents, members of the ERA Strategy committee and interested activists to dicuss the issue and draft language for a new ERA. At the ERA Summit, NOW President, Patricia Ireland

Chronology of the Equal Rights Amendment

The National Organization for Women site features a timeline of the Equal Rights Amendment, which begins in 1923, when Alice Paul drafted the original document. Learn more about women's continuing efforts to achieve equality by amending the Constitution.

Access this Web site from http://www.myreportlinks.com

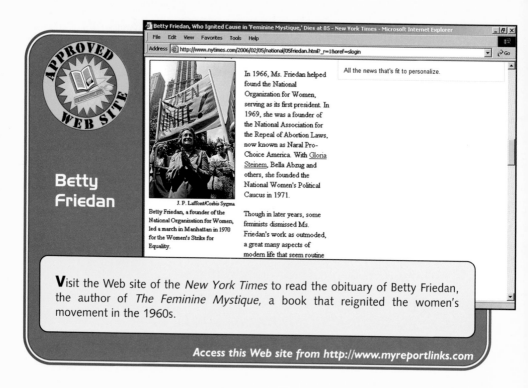

Betty Friedan, Who Ignited Cause in 'Feminine Mystique,' Dies at 85 - New York Times - Microsoft Internet Explorer

File   Edit   View   Favorites   Tools   Help

Address http://www.nytimes.com/2006/02/05/national/05friedan.html?_r=1&oref=slogin   Go

In 1966, Ms. Friedan helped found the National Organization for Women, serving as its first president. In 1969, she was a founder of the National Association for the Repeal of Abortion Laws, now known as Naral Pro-Choice America. With Gloria Steinem, Bella Abzug and others, she founded the National Women's Political Caucus in 1971.

All the news that's fit to personalize.

J. P. Laffont/Corbis Sygma
Betty Friedan, a founder of the National Organization for Women, led a march in Manhattan in 1970 for the Women's Strike for Equality.

Though in later years, some feminists dismissed Ms. Friedan's work as outmoded, a great many aspects of modern life that seem routine

Betty Friedan

Visit the Web site of the *New York Times* to read the obituary of Betty Friedan, the author of *The Feminine Mystique,* a book that reignited the women's movement in the 1960s.

Access this Web site from http://www.myreportlinks.com

→ WOMEN IN POLITICS

In 1916, the first woman, Jeanette Rankin of Montana, was elected to serve in Congress. Since the 1970s, the number of women holding political office at the local, state, and national levels has risen dramatically. In 1975, Ella Grasso of Connecticut became the first woman elected governor. A record number of women now serve in Congress as representatives and senators. As of the November 2006 midterm elections, there were eighty-seven women serving—seventy-one in the House and sixteen in the Senate.[1]

In 2006, Nancy Pelosi of California became the first woman to become Speaker of the U.S. House of Representatives. In this powerful position, she would become second in line for the presidency. According to the Constitution, should both the president and vice president be unable to perform their duties, the Speaker of the House assumes the presidency.

Although women are rising in the ranks, there are still gender gaps. The United States has not yet had a female president or vice-president. In 1984, Democrat Geraldine Ferraro became the first woman from a major political party to be nominated as a candidate for vice-president of the United States. Emphasizing that women can lead, Ferraro once said in a speech: "Some leaders are

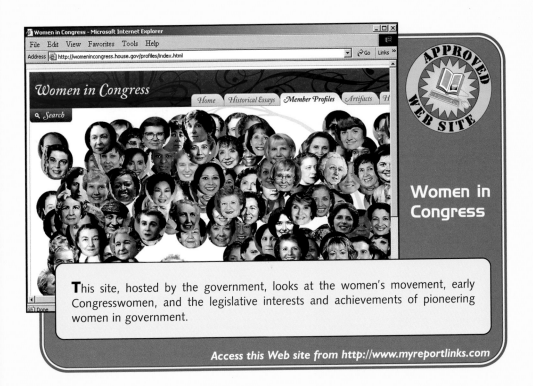

Women in Congress

This site, hosted by the government, looks at the women's movement, early Congresswomen, and the legislative interests and achievements of pioneering women in government.

Access this Web site from http://www.myreportlinks.com

born women."[2] In 2007, Senator Hillary Clinton of New York announced she would run to become the first female president of the United States.

➡ HOW DO WOMEN VOTE?

The Nineteenth Amendment more than doubled the number of people eligible to vote. According to the U.S. Census, in the presidential election of November 2004, a record 126 million people voted; this was out of a total of 215 million eligible voters. Voter turnout increased by 15 million voters from the election in 2000.[3]

The same report shows that women have been more likely than men to vote. In the November 2004 election, of the 111 million eligible female voters, 67.2 million voted. Of the 103 million eligible male voters, 58.4 million voted. In other words, a greater percentage of eligible women (65 percent) voted compared to eligible men (62 percent).[4]

◀ *In 1984, Congresswoman Geraldine Ferraro, from New York, became the first woman nominated by either the Republican or Democratic Parties to run for vice president. Ferraro and her running mate, Walter Mondale, lost the general election to Ronald Reagan and George H. W. Bush.*

▲ *In 2007, after eight years in the White House as first lady and having twice been elected to the U.S. Senate to represent New York, Hillary Clinton announced her intention to seek the Democratic Party's nomination to run for President.*

Until the presidential election of 1980, more men voted than women. In 1980, while more women voted than men,[5] a higher percentage of men voted for Ronald Reagan. This was the first time a gender gap appeared in voting, showing that women were indeed an independent voting force.

Sadly, despite the sacrifices women made to earn this right, many women never even register to vote. According to a recent survey, there were 22 million unmarried women, eighteen and older, who did not vote in the 2000 election.[6] What would Elizabeth Cady Stanton, Susan B. Anthony,

Alice Paul and Lucy Burns say about the way American women use or do not use their right to vote? These women had allowed themselves to be humiliated, beaten, and imprisoned, so that all women could enjoy this basic right.

➔What Does the Future Hold?

What does the U.S. Constitution mean for women in the twenty-first century? Like every new era, this one ushers in new challenges that society needs to address. Are there real differences between men and women and their needs in society?

Women have made remarkable progress since Seneca Falls, when the founding sisters claimed "all the rights and privileges which belong to them as citizens." But the Constitution does not protect women in all areas of life. Some issues remain unresolved—including gender discrimination, divorce and property rights, and privacy rights. Women still lag behind and earn less than men for similar work. Other contemporary issues to be tackled include sexual harassment, abortion, gay marriage, stem-cell research, and affirmative action.

The Constitution is a living document. "Women—left out when it was written—had to fight their way in through amendment, political action, and constitutional law cases."[7] The Constitution has shifted over time to reflect the changing relationships between men and women. It has been evolving over the last two hundred years, and it will continue to meet the needs of women and address their concerns. The Nineteenth Amendment no longer plays a role in how the United States Constitution is interpreted. Equality before the law is now a basic principle, but the battle for equal rights is far from over.

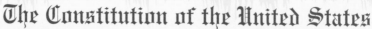

The Constitution of the United States

The text of the Constitution is presented here. All words are given their modern spelling and capitalization. Brackets [ ] indicate parts that have been changed or set aside by amendments.

Preamble

We the People of the United States, in Order to form a more perfect Union, establish Justice, insure domestic Tranquillity, provide for the common defence, promote the general Welfare, and secure the Blessings of Liberty to ourselves and our Posterity, do ordain and establish this Constitution for the United States of America.

Article I
The Legislative Branch

Section 1. All legislative powers herein granted shall be vested in a Congress of the United States, which shall consist of a Senate and House of Representatives.

The House of Representatives

Section 2. The House of Representatives shall be composed of members chosen every second year by the people of the several states, and the electors in each state shall have the qualifications requisite for electors of the most numerous branch of the state legislature.

No person shall be a Representative who shall not have attained to the age of twenty five years, and been seven years a citizen of the United States, and who shall not, when elected, be an inhabitant of that state in which he shall be chosen.

Representatives and direct taxes shall be apportioned among the several states which may be included within this union, according to their respective numbers, [which shall be determined by adding to the whole number of free persons, including those bound to service for a term of years, and excluding Indians not taxed, three fifths of all other persons]. The actual Enumeration shall be made within three years after the first meeting of the Congress of the United States, and within every subsequent term of ten years, in such manner as they shall by law direct. The number of Representatives shall not exceed one for every thirty thousand, but each state shall have at least one Representative; [and until such enumeration shall be made, the state of New Hampshire shall be entitled to chuse three, Massachusetts eight, Rhode Island and Providence Plantations one, Connecticut five, New York six, New Jersey four, Pennsylvania eight, Delaware one, Maryland six, Virginia ten, North Carolina five, South Carolina five, and Georgia three].

When vacancies happen in the Representation from any state, the executive authority thereof shall issue writs of election to fill such vacancies.

The House of Representatives shall choose their speaker and other officers; and shall have the sole power of impeachment.

The Senate

Section 3. The Senate of the United States shall be composed of two Senators from each state, [chosen by the legislature thereof,] for six years; and each Senator shall have one vote.

Immediately after they shall be assembled in consequence of the first election, they shall be divided as equally as may be into three classes. The seats of the Senators of the first class shall be vacated at the expiration of the second year, of the second class at the expiration of the fourth year, and the third class at the expiration of the sixth year, so that one third may be chosen every second year; [and if vacancies happen by resignation, or otherwise, during the recess of the legislature of any state, the executive thereof may make temporary appointments until the next meeting of the legislature, which shall then fill such vacancies].

No person shall be a Senator who shall not have attained to the age of thirty years, and been nine years a citizen of the United States and who shall not, when elected, be an inhabitant of that state for which he shall be chosen.

The Vice President of the United States shall be President of the Senate, but shall have no vote, unless they be equally divided.

The Senate shall choose their other officers, and also a President pro tempore, in the absence of the Vice President, or when he shall exercise the office of President of the United States.

The Senate shall have the sole power to try all impeachments. When sitting for that purpose, they shall be on oath or affirmation. When the President of the United States is tried, the Chief Justice shall preside: And no person shall be convicted without the concurrence of two thirds of the members present.

Judgment in cases of impeachment shall not extend further than to removal from office, and disqualification to hold and enjoy any office of honor, trust or profit under the United States: but the party convicted shall nevertheless be liable and subject to indictment, trial, judgment and punishment, according to law.

Organization of Congress

Section 4. The times, places and manner of holding elections for Senators and Representatives, shall be prescribed in each state by the legislature thereof; but the Congress may at any time by law make or alter such regulations, [except as to the places of choosing senators].

The Congress shall assemble at least once in every year, [and such meeting shall be on the first Monday in December], unless they shall by law appoint a different day.

Section 5. Each House shall be the judge of the elections, returns and qualifications of its own members, and a majority of each shall constitute a quorum to do business; but a smaller number may adjourn from day to day, and may be authorized to compel the attendance of absent members, in such manner, and under such penalties as each House may provide.

Each House may determine the rules of its proceedings, punish its members for disorderly behavior, and, with the concurrence of two thirds, expel a member.

Each House shall keep a journal of its proceedings, and from time to time publish the same, excepting such parts as may in their judgment require secrecy; and the yeas and nays of the members of either House on any question shall, at the desire of one fifth of those present, be entered on the journal.

Neither House, during the session of Congress, shall, without the consent of the other, adjourn for more than three days, nor to any other place than that in which the two Houses shall be sitting.

Section 6. The Senators and Representatives shall receive a compensation for their services, to be ascertained by law, and paid out of the treasury of the United States. They shall in all cases, except treason, felony and breach of the peace, be privileged from arrest during their attendance at the session of their respective Houses, and in going to and returning from the same; and for any speech or debate in either House, they shall not be questioned in any other place.

No Senator or Representative shall, during the time for which he was elected, be appointed to any civil office under the authority of the United States, which shall have been created, or the emoluments whereof shall have been increased during such time: and no person holding any office under the United States, shall be a member of either House during his continuance in office.

Section 7. All bills for raising revenue shall originate in the House of Representatives; but the Senate may propose or concur with amendments as on other Bills.

Every bill which shall have passed the House of Representatives and the Senate, shall, before it become a law, be presented to the President of the United States; if he approve he shall sign it, but if not he shall return it, with his objections to that House in which it shall have originated, who shall enter the objections at large on their journal, and proceed to reconsider it. If after such reconsideration two thirds of that House shall agree to pass the bill, it shall be sent, together with the objections, to the other House, by which it shall likewise be reconsidered, and if approved by two thirds of that House, it shall become a law. But in all such cases the votes of both Houses shall be determined by yeas and nays, and the names of the persons voting for and against the bill shall be entered on the journal of each House respectively. If any bill shall not be returned by the President within ten days (Sundays excepted) after it shall have been presented to him, the same shall be a law, in like manner as if he had signed it, unless the Congress by their adjournment prevent its return, in which case it shall not be a law.

Every order, resolution, or vote to which the concurrence of the Senate and House of Representatives may be necessary (except on a question of adjournment) shall be presented to the President of the United States; and before the same shall take effect, shall be approved by him, or being disapproved by him, shall be repassed by two thirds of the Senate and House of Representatives, according to the rules and limitations prescribed in the case of a bill.

Powers Granted to Congress
The Congress shall have the power:

Section 8. To lay and collect taxes, duties, imposts and excises, to pay the debts and provide for the common defense and general welfare of the United States; but all duties, imposts and excises shall be uniform throughout the United States;

To borrow money on the credit of the United States;

To regulate commerce with foreign nations, and among the several states, and with the Indian tribes;

To establish a uniform rule of naturalization, and uniform laws on the subject of bankruptcies throughout the United States;

To coin money, regulate the value thereof, and of foreign coin, and fix the standard of weights and measures;

To provide for the punishment of counterfeiting the securities and current coin of the United States;

To establish post offices and post roads;

To promote the progress of science and useful arts, by securing for limited times to authors and inventors the exclusive right to their respective writings and discoveries;

To constitute tribunals inferior to the Supreme Court;

To define and punish piracies and felonies committed on the high seas, and offenses against the law of nations;

To declare war, grant letters of marque and reprisal, and make rules concerning captures on land and water;

To raise and support armies, but no appropriation of money to that use shall be for a longer term than two years;

To provide and maintain a navy;

To make rules for the government and regulation of the land and naval forces;

To provide for calling forth the militia to execute the laws of the union, suppress insurrections and repel invasions;

To provide for organizing, arming, and disciplining, the militia, and for governing such part of them as may be employed in the service of the United States, reserving to the states respectively, the appointment of the officers, and the authority of training the militia according to the discipline prescribed by Congress;

To exercise exclusive legislation in all cases whatsoever, over such District (not exceeding ten miles square) as may, by cession of particular states, and the acceptance of Congress, become the seat of the government of the United States, and to exercise like authority over all places purchased by the consent of the legislature of the state in which the same shall be, for the erection of forts, magazines, arsenals, dockyards, and other needful buildings;—And

To make all laws which shall be necessary and proper for carrying into execution the foregoing powers, and all other powers vested by this Constitution in the government of the United States, or in any department or officer thereof.

Powers Forbidden to Congress

Section 9. The migration or importation of such persons as any of the states now existing shall think proper to admit, shall not be prohibited by the Congress prior to the year one thousand eight hundred and eight, but a tax or duty may be imposed on such importation, not exceeding ten dollars for each person.

The privilege of the writ of habeas corpus shall not be suspended, unless when in cases of rebellion or invasion the public safety may require it.

No bill of attainder or ex post facto law shall be passed.

No capitation, [or other direct,] tax shall be laid, unless in proportion to the census or enumeration herein before directed to be taken.

No tax or duty shall be laid on articles exported from any state.

No preference shall be given by any regulation of commerce or revenue to the ports of one state over those of another: nor shall vessels bound to, or from, one state, be obliged to enter, clear or pay duties in another.

No money shall be drawn from the treasury, but in consequence of appropriations made by law; and a regular statement and account of receipts and expenditures of all public money shall be published from time to time.

No title of nobility shall be granted by the United States: and no person holding any office of profit or trust under them, shall, without the consent of the Congress, accept of any present, emolument, office, or title, of any kind whatever, from any king, prince, or foreign state.

Powers Forbidden to the States

Section 10. No state shall enter into any treaty, alliance, or confederation; grant letters of marque and reprisal; coin money; emit bills of credit; make anything but gold and silver coin a tender in payment of debts; pass any bill of attainder, ex post facto law, or law impairing the obligation of contracts, or grant any title of nobility.

No state shall, without the consent of the Congress, lay any imposts or duties on imports or exports, except what may be absolutely necessary for executing its inspection laws: and the net produce of all duties and imposts, laid by any state on imports or exports, shall be for the use of the treasury of the United States; and all such laws shall be subject to the revision and control of the Congress.

No state shall, without the consent of Congress, lay any duty of tonnage, keep troops, or ships of war in time of peace, enter into any agreement or compact with another state, or with a foreign power, or engage in war, unless actually invaded, or in such imminent danger as will not admit of delay.

Article II
The Executive Branch

Section 1. The executive power shall be vested in a President of the United States of America. He shall hold his office during the term of four years, and, together with the Vice President, chosen for the same term, be elected, as follows:

Each state shall appoint, in such manner as the legislature thereof may direct, a number of electors, equal to the whole number of Senators and Representatives to which the State may be entitled in the Congress: but no Senator or Representative, or person holding an office of trust or profit under the United States, shall be appointed an elector.

[The electors shall meet in their respective states, and vote by ballot for two persons, of whom one at least shall not be an inhabitant of the same state with themselves. And they shall make a list of all the persons voted for, and of the number of votes for each; which list they shall sign and certify, and transmit sealed to the seat of the government of the United States, directed to the President of the Senate. The President of the Senate shall, in the presence of the Senate and House of Representatives, open all the certificates, and the votes shall then be counted. The person having the greatest number of votes shall be the President, if such number be a majority of the whole number of electors appointed; and if there be more than one who have such majority, and have an equal number of votes, then the House of Representatives shall immediately choose by ballot one of them for President; and if no person have a majority, then from the five highest on the list the said House shall in like manner choose the President. But in choosing the President, the votes shall be taken by States, the representation from each state having one vote; A quorum for this purpose shall consist of a member or members from two thirds of the states, and a majority of all the states shall be necessary to a choice. In every case, after the choice of the President, the person having the greatest number of votes of the electors shall be the Vice President. But if there should remain two or more who have equal votes, the Senate shall choose from them by ballot the Vice President.]

The Congress may determine the time of choosing the electors, and the day on which they shall give their votes; which day shall be the same throughout the United States.

No person except a natural born citizen, or a citizen of the United States, at the time of the adoption of this Constitution, shall be eligible to the office of President; neither shall any person be eligible to that office who shall not have attained to the age of thirty-five years, and been fourteen Years a resident within the United States.

In case of the removal of the President from office, or of his death, resignation, or inability to discharge the powers and duties of the said office, the same shall devolve on the Vice President, and the Congress may by law provide for the case of removal, death, resignation or inability, both of the President and Vice President, declaring what officer shall then act as President, and such officer shall act accordingly, until the disability be removed, or a President shall be elected.

The President shall, at stated times, receive for his services, a compensation, which shall neither be increased nor diminished during the period for which he shall have been elected, and he shall not receive within that period any other emolument from the United States, or any of them.

Before he enter on the execution of his office, he shall take the following oath or affirmation:—"I do solemnly swear (or affirm) that I will faithfully execute the office of President of the United States, and will to the best of my ability, preserve, protect and defend the Constitution of the United States."

Section 2. The President shall be commander-in-chief of the Army and Navy of the United States, and of the militia of the several states, when called into the actual service of the United States; he may require the opinion, in writing, of the principal officer in each of the executive departments, upon any subject relating to the duties of their respective offices, and he shall have power to grant reprieves and pardons for offenses against the United States, except in cases of impeachment.

He shall have power, by and with the advice and consent of the Senate, to make treaties, provided two-thirds of the Senators present concur; and he shall nominate, and by and with the advice and consent of the Senate, shall appoint ambassadors, other public ministers and consuls, judges of the Supreme Court, and all other officers of the United States, whose appointments are not herein otherwise provided for, and which shall be established by law: but the Congress may by law vest the appointment of such inferior officers, as they think proper, in the President alone, in the courts of law, or in the heads of departments.

The President shall have power to fill up all vacancies that may happen during the recess of the Senate, by granting commissions which shall expire at the end of their next session.

Section 3. He shall from time to time give to the Congress information of the state of the union, and recommend to their consideration such measures as he shall judge necessary and expedient; he may, on extraordinary occasions, convene both Houses, or either of them, and in case of disagreement between them, with respect to the time of adjournment, he may adjourn them to such time as he shall think proper; he shall receive ambassadors and other public ministers; he shall take care that the laws be faithfully executed, and shall commission all the officers of the United States.

Section 4. The President, Vice President and all civil officers of the United States, shall be removed from office on impeachment for, and conviction of, treason, bribery, or other high crimes and misdemeanors.

Article III
The Judicial Branch

Section 1. The judicial power of the United States, shall be vested in one Supreme Court, and in such inferior courts as the Congress may from time to time ordain and establish. The judges, both of the supreme and inferior courts, shall hold their offices during good behaviour, and shall, at stated times, receive for their services, a compensation, which shall not be diminished during their continuance in office.

Section 2. The judicial power shall extend to all cases, in law and equity, arising under this Constitution, the laws of the United States, and treaties made, or which shall be made, under their authority;—to all cases affecting ambassadors, other public ministers and consuls;—to all cases of admiralty and maritime jurisdiction, [—to controversies to which the United States shall be a party;—to controversies between two or more states, [between a state and citizens of another state;], between citizens of different states;—between citizens of the same state, claiming lands under grants of different states, and between a state, or the citizens thereof, and foreign states, [citizens or subjects].

In all cases affecting ambassadors, other public ministers and consuls, and those in which a state shall be party, the Supreme Court shall have original jurisdiction. In all the other cases before mentioned, the Supreme Court shall have appellate jurisdiction, both as to law and fact, with such exceptions, and under such regulations as the Congress shall make.

The trial of all crimes, except in cases of impeachment, shall be by jury; and such trial shall be held in the state where the said crimes shall have been committed; but when not committed within any state, the trial shall be at such place or places as the Congress may by law have directed.

Section 3. Treason against the United States, shall consist only in levying war against them, or in adhering to their enemies, giving them aid and comfort. No person shall be convicted of treason unless on the testimony of two witnesses to the same overt act, or on confession in open court.

The Congress shall have power to declare the punishment of treason, but no attainder of treason shall work corruption of blood, or forfeiture except during the life of the person attainted.

Article IV
Relation of the States to Each Other

Section 1. Full faith and credit shall be given in each state to the public acts, records, and judicial proceedings of every other state. And the Congress may by general laws prescribe the manner in which such acts, records, and proceedings shall be proved, and the effect thereof.

Section 2. The citizens of each state shall be entitled to all privileges and immunities of citizens in the several states.

A person charged in any state with treason, felony, or other crime, who shall flee from justice, and be found in another state, shall on demand of the executive authority of the state from which he fled, be delivered up, to be removed to the state having jurisdiction of the crime.

[No person held to service or labor in one state, under the laws thereof, escaping into another, shall, in consequence of any law or regulation therein, be discharged from such service or labor, but shall be delivered up on claim of the party to whom such service or labor may be due.]

Federal-State Relations

Section 3. New states may be admitted by the Congress into this Union; but no new states shall be formed or erected within the jurisdiction of any other state, nor any state be formed by the junction of two or more states, without the consent of the legislatures of the states concerned, as well as of the Congress.

The Congress shall have power to dispose of and make all needful rules and regulations respecting the territory or other property belonging to the United States; and nothing in this Constitution shall be so construed as to prejudice any claims of the United States, or of any particular state.

Section 4. The United States shall guarantee to every state in this union a republican form of government, and shall protect each of them against invasion; and on application of the legislature, or of the executive (when the legislature cannot be convened) against domestic violence.

Article V
Amending the Constitution

The Congress, whenever two thirds of both houses shall deem it necessary, shall propose amendments to this Constitution, or, on the application of the legislatures of two thirds of the several states, shall call a convention for proposing amendments, which, in either case, shall be valid to all intents and purposes, as part of this Constitution, when ratified by the legislatures of three fourths of the several states, or by conventions in three fourths thereof, as the one or the other mode of ratification may be proposed by the Congress; provided [that no amendment which may be made prior to the year one thousand eight hundred and eight shall in any manner affect the first and fourth clauses in the ninth section of the first article; and] that no state, without its consent, shall be deprived of its equal suffrage in the Senate.

Article VI
National Debts

All debts contracted and engagements entered into, before the adoption of this Constitution, shall be as valid against the United States under this Constitution, as under the Confederation.

Supremacy of the National Government

This Constitution, and the laws of the United States which shall be made in pursuance thereof; and all treaties made, or which shall be made, under the authority of the United States, shall be the supreme law of the land; and the judges in every state shall be bound thereby, anything in the constitution or laws of any State to the contrary notwithstanding.

The senators and representatives before mentioned, and the members of the several state legislatures, and all executive and judicial officers, both of the United States and of the several states, shall be bound by oath or affirmation, to support this Constitution; but no religious test shall ever be required as a qualification to any office or public trust under the United States.

Article VII
Ratifying the Constitution

The ratification of the conventions of nine states, shall be sufficient for the establishment of this Constitution between the states so ratifying the same.

Done in convention by the unanimous consent of the states present the seventeenth day of September in the year of our Lord one thousand seven hundred and eighty seven and of the independence of the United States of America the twelfth. In witness whereof we have hereunto subscribed our Names.

Amendment XIX

The right of citizens of the United States to vote shall not be denied or abridged by the United States or by any State on account of sex.

Congress shall have the power to enforce this article by appropriate legislation.

Report Links

The Internet sites described below can be accessed at http://www.myreportlinks.com

▶**Not For Ourselves Alone**
Editor's Choice PBS offers a glimpse into key events of the suffrage movement.

▶**The Charters of Freedom**
Editor's Choice Read the U.S. Constitution on the National Archives Web site.

▶**National Women's History Museum**
Editor's Choice This museum's Web site tells the story of women throughout American history.

▶**By Popular Demand: "Votes for Women" Suffrage Pictures**
Editor's Choice The Library of Congress presents a collection of suffrage photographs.

▶**Women's Rights National Historical Park**
Editor's Choice This National Park Service Web site provides an overview of the park.

▶**U.S. Constitution: Nineteenth Amendment**
Editor's Choice Text of the Nineteenth Amendment is available.

▶**American Civil Liberties Union**
The ACLU offers an overview of the struggle for women's rights in the United States.

▶**Alice Paul Institute**
Explore the life and legacy of Alice Paul.

▶**Alice Paul's Fight for Suffrage**
Learn about the fight for a woman's right to vote.

▶**American Experience**
This PBS Web site spotlights President Woodrow Wilson.

▶**The Barnard Center for Research on Women**
This organization works to promote feminist scholarship and activism.

▶**Betty Friedan**
This *New York Times* obituary looks at the life of Betty Friedan.

▶**Bradwell v. Illinois**
Learn more about Myra Bradwell's application to the Illinois state bar.

▶**Chronology of the Equal Rights Amendment**
The National Organization for Women (NOW) has a timeline of the ERA.

▶**The Equal Rights Amendment**
Visit this Web site to learn about the historic ERA.

Report Links

The Internet sites described below can be accessed at
http://www.myreportlinks.com

▶**Federal Voting Rights Laws**
The United States Department of Justice outlines the federal voting rights laws.

▶**Frederick Douglass**
The University of Rochester offers information on a leader of the abolitionist movement.

▶**A History of the American Suffragist Movement**
Visit this site for a history of suffrage activities in the United States.

▶**League of Women Voters**
Visit the site of this important grassroots organization.

▶**The Lucretia Coffin Mott Papers Project**
Pomona College presents an overview of Lucretia Coffin Mott's life.

▶**_Minor v. Happersett_**
This is a full-text copy of the Supreme Court decision.

▶**_The Narrative of Sojourner Truth_**
Learn more about abolitionist Sojourner Truth.

▶**The National Women's History Project**
This site chronicles the historic accomplishments of women.

▶**Places Where Women Made History**
The National Park Service commemorates women and the places where they made history.

▶**Suffrage Prisoners**
The Library of Congress presents the history of the suffrage movement.

▶**Susan B. Anthony House**
Learn about one of America's most important women and take a tour of the Anthony home.

▶**Twenty–Fourth Amendment**
Read the text of the Twenty–fourth Amendment.

▶**_U.S. v. Susan B. Anthony_**
This site provides a good overview of this historic Supreme Court case.

▶**Women in Congress**
This government Web site offers a history of women in Congress.

▶**Women's Suffrage**
This is a collection of suffrage photographs.

abolition—Movement to end slavery in the United States.

abolitionist—A person opposed to slavery.

American Equal Rights Association (AERA)—Founded in 1866 to combine the suffrage movement and the abolition movement in order to extend the vote to all adults.

American Women's Suffrage Association (AWSA)—An organization founded by Lucy Stone in 1869 that worked for women's suffrage on a state-by-state basis.

Anti-suffragist—A person opposed to extending the vote to women.

Declaration of Sentiments—Declaration of twelve resolutions for women's rights passed at the first Women's Rights Convention in 1848 in Seneca Falls, New York.

defendant—The person who is being sued in court.

Due Process of Law—A phrase in the Fourteenth Amendment that says an individual cannot be deprived of life, liberty, or property without legal procedures.

Equal Protection Clause—A phrase in the Fourteenth Amendment that requires states to guarantee the same rights, privileges, and protections to all citizens.

Equal Rights Amendment—An amendment written by Alice Paul in 1923 to secure equal rights for all women. It was never ratified.

Fifteenth Amendment—A Constitutional amendment passed in 1870 that granted the right to vote to all men, regardless of race.

Fourteenth Amendment—A Constitutional amendment adopted in 1868 that has the Due Process of Law Clause and Equal Protection Clause.

gender gap—A term used by the National Organization for Women to show that women vote differently from men.

grandfather clause—A law that allowed an individual to vote if his grandfather had voted.

literacy test—A reading and writing test an individual had to pass before being allowed to vote.

National American Woman Suffrage Association (NAWSA)— Formed when the National Women's Suffrage Association and the American Women's Suffrage Association combined in 1890. Members fought for women's suffrage at the state and national levels.

National Organization for Women (NOW)—A feminist organization founded in the 1960s.

National Woman's Party—Formed by Alice Paul, this party used radical methods in an effort to win the vote for women.

National Women's Suffrage Association (NWSA)—A radical organization founded by Elizabeth Cady Stanton and Susan B. Anthony to fight for women's suffrage.

oppression—Unjust or cruel exercise of authority or power.

picket—A peaceful way to protest in which individuals gather outside a workplace and carry signs to gain public attention for their cause. Also an individual who engages in that activity.

plaintiff—The person who is suing in court.

poll tax—A state tax that an individual had to pay before being allowed to vote.

racism—The belief that some races are superior to others.

ratify—To formally approve something.

reform—An attempt to change society for the better.

Silent Sentinels—Women from the National Woman's Party who picketed outside the White House. They rarely spoke and carried banners as a form of protest.

suffrage—The right to vote.

suffragist—A person who is working to gain voting rights for women.

Thirteenth Amendment—A Constitutional amendment adopted in 1865 that abolished slavery.

Women's Political Union—Founded as the Equality League of Self-Supporting Women in 1907 by Harriot Stanton Blatch, renamed in 1910.

writ of habeas corpus—Authorization to bring a person to court before a judge.

Chapter 1. They Suffered for Suffrage

1. Linda G. Ford, *Iron-Jawed Angels: The Suffrage Militancy of the National Woman's Party, 1912–1920* (Lanham, Md.: University Press of America, Inc., 1991), p. 180.

2. "Suffragists Speak: 1910–1920, A Multi-Media Resource," *SIMS, UC Berkeley,* 1998, <http://www2.sims.berkeley.edu/courses /is290-2/f98/GroupC/SuffragistsSpeak/primarybooks/story1 .txt> (February 9, 2007).

3. Doris Stevens, *Jailed for Freedom: American Women Win the Vote* (Troutdale, Ore.: NewSage Press, 1995), p. 123.

4. Ford, p. 180.

5. *Suffragists Speak: 1910–1920.*

6. Ibid.

7. "White House Pickets Held Without Bail," *The Washington Post,* Washington, D.C., November 14, 1917.

8. Ford, p. 181.

Chapter 2. "Failure Is Impossible"

1. Jethro K. Lieberman, *The Evolving Constitution: How the Supreme Court Has Ruled on Issues From Abortion to Zoning* (New York: Random House, 1992), p. 563.

2. Ibid.

3. "Visit the Homestead of Lucy Stone," *West Brookfield Historical Commission,* n.d., <http://westbrookfield.org/lucystone .htm> (March 1, 2007).

4. Eleanor Flexner, *Century of Struggle: The Woman's Rights Movement in the United States* (Cambridge, Mass.: The Belknap Press of Harvard University Press, 1975), p. 63.

5. Ibid., p. 15.

6. Eleanor Clift, *Founding Sisters and the Nineteenth Amendment* (Hoboken, N.J.: John Wiley & Sons, Inc., 2003), p. 28.

7. Geoffrey C. Ward, *Not for Ourselves Alone: The Story of Elizabeth Cady Stanton and Susan B. Anthony* (New York: Alfred A. Knopf, 1999), p. 6.

8. Elizabeth Frost-Knappman and Kathryn Cullen-DuPont, *Women's Suffrage in America: An Eyewitness History* (New York: Facts On File, 2005), p. 169.

9. Frederick Douglass and Philip S. Foner, ed., *Frederick Douglass on Women's Rights* (New York: Da Capo Press, 1992), p. 33.

10. Ibid., p. 87.

11. Rosemary H. Knower, "Teaching With Documents: Woman Suffrage and the 19th Amendment: Failure Is Impossible, *United States National Archives and Records Administration,* 1995, <http://www.archives.gov/education/lessons/woman-suffrage /script.html?template=print> (March 1, 2007).

12. Frost-Knappman and Cullen-Dupont, p. 174.

13. Ibid., p. 190.

14. "The Progress of Colored Women: by Mary Church Terrell," *American Memory, Library of Congress,* n.d. <http://memory.loc.gov/cgi-bin/query/r?asmmem/murray:@field (DOCID+@lit(lcrbmrpt0a13div2))> (January 27, 2007).

15. Frost-Knappman and Cullen-Dupont, p. 243.

16. Knower.

17. Francis Parkman, *Some of the Reasons Against Woman Suffrage* (Northridge, Calif.: Santa Susana Press, California State University, 1977), pp. 3–7.

18. Susan E. Marshall, *Splintered Sisterhood: Gender and Class in the Campaign Against Woman Suffrage* (Madison, Wis.: University of Wisconsin Press, 1997), p. 5.

19. Knower.

20. Lynn Sherr, *Failure Is Impossible: Susan B. Anthony in Her Own Words* (New York: Random House, 1995), p. 324.

21. Rosalyn Terborg-Penn, *African American Women in the Struggle for the Vote, 1850–1920* (Bloomington, Ind.: Indiana University Press, 1998). pp. 121–123.

22. Frost-Knappman and Cullen-Dupont, p. 315.

23. Doris Stevens, *Jailed for Freedom* (Troutdale, Ore.: NewSage Press, 1995), p.75.

24. Ibid., p. 88.

25. Ibid.

26. Ibid., p. 96.

27. Linda G. Ford, *Iron-Jawed Angels: The Suffrage Militancy of the National Woman's Party, 1912–1920* (Lanham, Md.: University Press of America, 1991). p. 198.

28. Clift, p. 144.

29. Stevens, pp. 113–114.

30. Ibid., p. 116.

31. Ford, p. 182.

32. "Ideas and Strategies of the Woman Suffrage Movement, Document #48," *UC Davis,* n.d., <http://marchand.ucdavis.edu/lessons/suffrage/suffrage.html> (March 1, 2007).

33. Stevens, p. 125.

34. Ibid., p. 160.

35. Ibid., p. 177.

36. Frost-Knappman and Cullen-Dupont, p. 335.

37. Tonya Bolden, ed., *33 Things Every Girl Should Know About Women's History* (New York: Crown Publishers, 2002), p. 45.

Chapter 3. What Does the Nineteenth Amendment Mean?

1. Michael S. Lief and H. Mitchell Caldwell, *And the Walls Came Tumbling Down: Closing Arguments That Changed the Way We Live* (New York: A Lisa Drew Book/Scribner, 2004), p. 199.

2. Felice D. Gordon, *After Winning: The Legacy of the New Jersey Suffragists, 1920—1947* (New Brunswick, N.J.: Rutgers University Press, 1986), pp. 8–9.

3. Frances J. Bjorkman and Annie G. Porritt, eds., "'The Blue Book,' Woman suffrage, history, arguments and results," *Library of Congress: American Memory,* n.d.,<http://memory.loc.gov/cgi-bin /query/r?ammem/naw:@field(DOCID+@lit(rbnawsan4862div 163))> (March 5, 2007).

4. Reva B. Siegel, "She the People: The Nineteenth Amendment, Sex Equality, Federalism, and the Family," *Yale Law School, Public Law & Legal Theory Research Paper No. 12,* n.d., <http://papers.ssrn.com/sol3/papers.cfm?abstract_id=296784> (March 5, 2007).

5. Ibid.

6. Ibid.

7. Carrie Chapman Catt and Nettie Rogers Shuler, "Woman Suffrage and politics; the inner story of the suffrage movement," *Library of Congress: American Memory,* n.d., <http://memory.loc .gov/cgi-bin/query/r?ammem/naw:@field(DOCID+@ lit(rbnawsan6874div38))> (March 5, 2007).

8. Siegel.

Chapter 4. Testing the Limits

1. Barbara Allen Babcock, "Book Review: Feminist Lawyers," as published in Stanford Law Review: Feminist Lawyers, vol. 50: 1689, May 1989, *Women's Legal History Biography Project, Stanford Law School,* n.d., <http://womenslegalhistory.stanford .edu/articles/h1femini.htm> (March 5, 2007).

2. *Bradwell v. The State,* "83 U.S. 130," <http://www.lexis .com/research/retrieve?_m=db9d3be47149eb154e1c2b16159238e8 &_browseType=TEXTONLY&docnum=2&_fmtstr=FULL&_startdoc =1&wchp=dGLbVzb-zSkAB&_md5=ffdc461af5917818 573568d5dcfa7626> (February 15, 2007).

3. Supreme Court of the United States, *"Minor v. Happersett,* 88 U.S. 162," October, 1874, *University of Missouri-Kansas City School of Law,* n.d., <http://www.law.umkc.edu/faculty/projects /ftrials/conlaw/minorvhapp.html> (March 5, 2007).

4. Doug Linder, "The Trial of Susan B. Anthony for Illegal Voting," *Famous American Trials-University of Missouri-Kansas City School of Law,* 2001, <http://www.law.umkc.edu/faculty/projects /ftrials/anthony/sbaaccount.html> (March 5, 2007).

5. Ibid.

6. Ibid.

7. Michael S. Lief and H. Mitchell Caldwell, *And the Walls Came Tumbling Down: Closing Arguments That Changed the Way We Live* (New York: A Lisa Drew Book/Scribner, 2004), pp. 197–198.

8. Ibid., p. 200.

9. "Jeff J. Harland v. Territory of Washington, 3 Wash. Terr. 131," 1887, <http://www.lexis.com/research/retrieve/frames ?_m=aa8298a75afa6bc7dd016b31c327a921&csvc=bl&cform= byName&_fmtstr=FULL&docnum=1&_startdoc=1&wchp= dGLbVtb-zSkAV&_md5=399fbe96617cb57fc20eb6362a21bbd0> (February 11, 2007).

10. U.S. Supreme Court, "Leser v. Garnett, 258 U.S. 130 (1922)," *FindLaw,* n.d., <http://caselaw.lp.findlaw.com/scripts/printer_ friendly.pl?page=us/258/130.html> (March 5, 2007).

11. "The U.S. Constitution: Nineteenth Amendment," *FindLaw,* n.d., <http://caselaw.lp.findlaw.com/data/constitution /amendment19/> (March 5, 2007).

12. "Breedlove v. Suttles, 302 U.S. 277 (1937)," *FindLaw,* n.d., <http://caselaw.lp.findlaw.com/scripts/getcase.pl?navby =case&court=us&vol=302&invol=277> (October 1, 2006).

13. U.S. Supreme Court, "Harper v. Virginia State Board of Elections, 383 U.S. 663 (1966)," *Justia.com,* n.d., <http://supreme .justia.com/us/383/663/case.html> (March 5, 2007).

14. U.S. Supreme Court, "Lassiter v. Northampton County Board of Elections, 360 U.S. 45 (1959)," *Justia.com,* n.d., <http:// supreme.justia.com/us/360/45/case.html> (March 5, 2007).

Chapter 5. A Living Document

1. Joyce L. Broussard, "The Court and Gender," *The History of the Supreme Court,* n.d., <http://www.historyofsupremecourt .org/history/gender/overviewessay.htm> (March 5, 2007).

2. Ibid.

3. U.S. Supreme Court, "Glasser v. United States, 315 U.S. 60 (1942)," *vLex.us,* n.d., <http://www.vlex.us/caselaw/U-S-Supreme-Court/Glasser-v-United-States-315-U-S-60-1942/2100-20014440,01.html>(March 5, 2007).

4. Linda K. Kerber, *No Constitutional Right to Be Ladies: Women and the Obligations of Citizenship* (New York: Hill and Wang, 1998), pp. 177–183.

5. Ibid., pp. 209–217.

6. *Mrs. Lorena W. Weeks v. Southern Bell Telephone & Telegraph Co.* "408F.2nd 228". 1969. <https://www.lexis.com/research

/retrieve/frames?_m=95dba20a04bc17e553ad38ed15fb9988&csvc
=bl&cform=byName&_fmtstr=FULL&docnum=1&_startdoc
=1&wchp=dGLzVzz-zSkAB&_md5=72be3b1585fd0
eae8c340ee0daf55793> (February 6, 2007).

7. Clare Cushman, ed., from *Supreme Court Decisions & Women's Rights-Milestones to Equality,* " Breaking New Ground: Reed v. Reed, 404 U.S. 71 (1971)," *The Supreme Court Historical Society,* September 26, 2006, <http://www.supremecourthistory.org/05_ learning/subs/05_e01.html> (April 4, 2008).

8. U.S. Supreme Court, "Rostker v. Goldberg, 453 U.S. 57 (1981)," *OYEZ.org,* n.d., <http://www.oyez.org/cases/case /?case=1980–1989/1980/1980_80_251> (March 5, 2007).

9. U.S. Supreme Court, "Roberts v. United States Jaycees, 468 U.S. 609 (1984)," *OYEZ.org,* n.d., <http://www.oyez.org/cases/case /?case=1980–1989/1983/1983_83_724> (March 5, 2007).

10. Sibyl A. Schwarzenbach and Patricia Smith, eds., *Women and the United States Constitution: History, Interpretation, and Practice* (New York: Columbia University Press, 2003), pp. 335–346.

Chapter 6. Do Women Really Have the Same Rights as Men?

1. Lea Terhune, "U.S. Midterm Elections Increase Women's Congressional Clout," *USINFO: United States Department of State,* November 17, 2006, <http://usinfo.state.gov/xarchives/display .html?p=washfile-english&y=2006&m=November&x= 20061117145152mlenuhret9.807986e-02> (March 5, 2007).

2. Tonya Bolden, *33 Things Every Girl Should Know About Women's History* (New York: Crown Publishers, 2002), p. 66.

3. Kelly Holder as published in the *U.S. Census Bureau,* "Voting and Registration in the Election of November 2004," *U.S. Department of Commerce,* March 2006, <www.census.gov/prod/2006pubs/p20-556.pdf> (March 5, 2007).

4. Ibid.

5. Eleanor Clift, *Founding Sisters and the Nineteenth Amendment* (Hoboken, N.J.: John Wiley & Sons, 2003), p. 6.

6. NOW with David Brancaccio, "Politics and Economy: Women and the Vote, Gender Gap?" *PBS,* October 15, 2004, <http:// www.pbs.org/now/politics/gendergap.html> (March 5, 2007).

7. Jean Bickmore White, "Women and the Constitution: After Two Hundred Years," as published in Weber Studies journal, vol. 5.2, Fall 1998, *Weber State University,* n.d., <http://weberstudies .weber.edu/archive/archive%20A%20%20Vol.%201-10.3/Vol .%205.2/5.2White.htm> (March 5, 2007).

Adams, Colleen. *Woman's Suffrage: A Primary Source History.* New York: Rosen, 2003.

Bausum, Ann. *With Courage and Cloth: Winning the Fight for a Woman's Right to Vote.* Washington, D.C.: National Geographic, 2004.

Bohannon, Lisa Frederiksen. *Failure Is Impossible: The Story of Susan B. Anthony.* Greensboro, N.C.: Morgan Reynolds, 2002.

Dumbeck, Kristina. *Leaders of Women's Suffrage.* San Diego, Calif.: Lucent Books, 2001.

Keller, Fristin Thoennes. *Carrie Chapman Catt: A Voice for Women.* Minneapolis: Compass Point Books, 2006.

Kops, Deborah. *Women's Suffrage.* San Diego, Calif.: Blackbirch Press, 2004.

Raumm, Elizabeth. *Alice Paul.* Chicago: Heinemann Library, 2004.

Rossi, Ann. *Created Equal: Women Campaign for the Right to Vote: 1840–1920.* Washington, D.C.: National Geographic Society, 2005.

Somervill, Barbara A. *Votes for Women! The Story of Carrie Chapman Catt.* Greensboro, N.C.: Morgan Reynolds, 2003.